Speaking
OF
Nature

Speaking

O

For Mary & John

May you always find
beauty in Nature.

Bill Davidson

Nature

BILL DANIELSON

with photographs and illustrations
by the author

FRONT COVER: Tree Swallows.

BACK COVER (CLOCKWISE FROM TOP): Common Raven; Round-lobed Hepatica; Sunset at Bog Pond, Savoy, Massachusetts; Male American Toad.

Published by
William Danielson, naturalist/author/photographer/illustrator
227 Franklin Street, Suite A
North Adams, MA 01247
wrdanie@attglobal.net
www.speakingofnature.com

Printed in the United States of America by Daaman Printing.

Cover and text design and production by Jeff Potter, Potter Publishing Studio
Back cover author photograph by John Danielson

ISBN 0-9714904-9-X

5 4 3 2 1

For Glove

Table of Contents

Introduction vii

SPRING

The Red-Winged Blackbird *3*

    The Spring Peeper, 11

    Skunk Cabbage, 16

    Shrews, 20

    The Eastern Phoebe, 25

    Spring Wildflowers, 30

    The Garter Snake, 36

SUMMER

Canoeing *43*

    Ferns, 49

    The Common Clearwing, 53

    The American Beaver, 57

    The American Toad, 62

    The Painted Turtle, 66

    The Northern Pitcher Plant, 73

FALL

Life's Big Questions. *79*

    Nuthatch Evolution, 84

    Burdocks, 88

    The Eastern Chipmunk, 92

    The Broad-Winged Hawk, 96

    The Blue Jay, 100

    The Monarch Butterfly, 104

WINTER

Signs of Winter *109*

    The Red Squirrel, 115

    Poison Ivy, 119

    The Common Raven, 123

    The American Crow, 128

    Lichens, 133

    Cattails, 138

Introduction

A S FAR AS WE CAN TELL, the Earth is something on the order of 4.5 billion years old. Actually, that isn't too impressive without all of the zeros, so let me try again.

Ready? As far as we can tell, the Earth is something on the order of 4,500,000,000 years old. If you do the math you will see that this breaks down to 4,500,000 millennia, or 45,000,000 centuries. I'll share a little secret with you: that's really old.

In that time the Earth has witnessed and endured many changes. The surface temperatures of what was once a ball of molten rock and metals cooled, an atmosphere formed, meteors fell, the continents drifted, and a thin membrane of life spread tenuously across the planet's surface. Great creatures rose and fell, great calamities came and went, and through it all one thing remained constant — time. No matter what happened, time went on.

About 50,000 centuries ago a new life form began to emerge. Evolution conducted its experiments, taking the original form and breaking it into different variations. Some worked, others didn't, and eventually a refined and well-adapted animal took shape.

The first version learned to use tools, and was later given the designation *Homo habilis,* meaning "Handy Man." The next version could use tools, but also stood erect, and was given the designation *Homo erectus.* The present version, third in a line of who knows how many, came forth about 2,000 centuries ago. It could use tools, it stood erect, and it was smart. It was so smart, in fact, that it named itself; the name it chose was Homo sapiens, or "Wise Man."

I wonder, though, if the name "Wise Man" might have been a bit premature. Perhaps "Smart Man," or "Clever Man" would have been better. We certainly are clever, but there are times when I doubt that we hold any wisdom within us at all.

Humans have only been around in our present form for the last 2,000 centuries. Put another way, we humans have only been on Earth for the last 0.004 percent of its existence. Up until our arrival, the world got along just fine. Since our arrival, the world has managed to get by pretty well. And should we ever disappear, the world will get along just fine.

Of course, I am using geologic time as a reference, and I am thinking in the long-term. The problem is that humans do not live on the geological time scale. Few of us live for a full century, and even if we do, we only live as energetic, healthy adults for about 50 years.

In that time we want things to go our way. We might want that new car, or that fancy pair of shoes, and we might be willing to do anything to get them. As a result, we usually think only in the shortest of short-terms. This is where we run into trouble. Our lives are simply too short to allow us to see the ramifications of everything we do. Yet while we may not notice the damage we do to our environment, our children (and their children) most certainly will. Then of course there are the millions of different plants and animals that live on Earth with us — that silent majority of living things that cannot protest whenever we do something stupid.

Yet even though we live such short lives, we are smart enough to consider the ramifications of our actions without actually having to witness the results first hand. We are learning to do this because we, the children of our grandparents' children, have seen the ramifications of the actions of the last century.

At the beginning of the 20th Century humanity had the notion that the world was ours to do with as we pleased. We also had a particularly stupid outlook toward animals. As an example, let me share a little passage from a newspaper called the Shelburne Falls Messenger:

Dated October 9, 1912, the topic of conversation was owls — "The whole owl family has likewise been arraigned by the biological survey court, rigorously tried, and finally discharged with the exception of a single individual. The old horned owl of the forest is in reality an outlaw. He sits in the depths of his forest and broods. His wisdom and his brooding have caused him to become unduly melancholy and he has grown vindictive against his rival in wisdom, man. To avenge himself upon his rival, he makes haste to devastate whatever chicken roosts may lie in his path."

This, I hope you will agree, is one of the most idiotic things I have ever heard. To even suggest that owls seek out and destroy chickens because they are mad at people is just too loony to even consider. I cannot even comprehend the mind that came up with such a statement.

Today, some 90 years later, we are using our brains a little better. We now know that owls are just owls. Some are large, some are small, and they are all beautiful birds of prey that will eat anything they can catch and kill. Owls do not seek vengeance upon us, or our chickens, for anything, and we have stopped shooting them. Unfortunately, there are many other animals that we still persecute.

In December of 1999 a very disturbing Associated Press story appeared in newspapers across the country. In it, we learned that

West Coast salmon fishermen wanted to start shooting seals and sea lions because they believed the marine mammals were eating all of the salmon. They didn't seem to want to consider the fact that the salmon, the seals, and the sea lions all managed to flourish before we humans started killing them all en masse. The ultimate reasons behind shooting seals and sea lions were money and greed, and that is a shame.

We need to learn to respect owls, sea lions, blue jays, hummingbirds, oak trees, water lilies, chipmunks, and the rest of our neighbors on Earth. We have to learn to consider them on a daily basis, and we have to try to make the decisions in our lives while keeping them in mind. Only when we can do this do we deserve the designation of "Wise Man."

I have been greatly privileged to be able to spend a substantial portion of my life studying nature and the environment. When I share my experiences through writing I try to help people look at the world in a different way. In the process I myself routinely learn something new, which makes me a better advocate for the plants and animals I write about. My goal, one that I think is very important, is to help us all to become wiser, gentler, and more considerate people.

This book is a collection of those essays that have had the greatest responses from my friends. Some of the topics are well worn, others may be new to you, but I hope you are able to discover something new in each one — something that you never knew before and something you can share with a friend or loved one. Whether you are a friend of mine from way back when, or a person who is just getting to know me, I can only hope that you will understand and appreciate the things I am trying to share with you.

One final thought before I continue on. Do you remember all of the fuss that surrounded the changing of the calendars from the

1900's to the 2000's? Do you remember the hysteria and the merchandising? Perhaps you even have a complete set of Y2K flashlights in your closet at home — unopened and collecting dust? Well I will give you this little bit of advice that you can carry with you to every New Year and every New Day for that matter: Don't worry! 45 million centuries have already come and gone, and one more won't make much of a difference. The year on the calendar is a human artifact and has little effect on life.

As far as the Earth is concerned it is the year 4,500,000,000 and change. Believe me when I tell you that there isn't a herring gull in the world that cares what year it is. They are supremely indifferent to such trivial things. As long as we are close to the ones we love, and as long as we treat others (birds, mammals, plants, people, etc.) with kindness and courtesy, everything will be just fine. After all, we're all in this together.

—*Bill Danielson,*
Buckland, Massachusetts

Speaking OF Nature

SPRING

The Red-Winged Blackbird

THE RAINY DAYS OF APRIL are some of my favorite days of the year. Gray skies, warm air, all of the promise of the coming bloom of life, and a gentle, steady rain — these are good days for walking along favorite trails and taking one last look at the landscape before everything turns green.

You might follow a trail that wanders past a beaver pond, find a spot where you can sit without getting too wet, lean against a tree, and relax for a while. And as you sit by this small country pond a typical springtime scene might unfold before you.

A pair of Canada geese quietly paddles along the far shore, aware of your presence but only mildly interested. There would be no frogs out yet, nor would there be any dragonflies, water beetles, newts or water lilies, but one of spring's most marvelous heralds would be present in all his glory. Wearing a jet-black uniform with the bright red and yellow badges of his office, a male red-winged blackbird would fly from one side of the pond to another and sing reveille, impatient for the world to wake up.

Okay, I'll admit this is a slightly romantic notion, but there is no arguing that red-winged blackbirds are truly impressive little birds. I love watching male birds sing and male red-winged blackbirds put on a wonderful show. The best thing about male redwings, however, is that they will sing and display out in the open.

The red-winged blackbird *(Agelaius phoeniceus)* is probably pretty well known by most people, but perhaps I should say that the male is well known. These jet-black birds, with their red and yellow epaulets, are noisy, brassy birds that will set up shop in the marsh, or wet field, just down the road. In fact, male red-winged blackbirds will even set up territories in drainage ditches that have standing water and a few cattails. They are beautiful birds with complex social lives, but how well do we know them? I think you would be surprised by what you don't know about a such a well-known bird.

To help you better understand the lives of red-winged blackbirds let me tell you the story of a typical male red-winged blackbird's summer. To preserve the anonymity of my sources, and thus avoid an embarrassing lawsuit, let's just call this particular red-winged blackbird. . . oh, Carl.

Now Carl probably spent the winter in more southern latitudes with many other species of blackbirds. It is even possible that Carl headed out to the Caribbean Islands, but eventually he got the itch to head north again. Travelling in large flocks, red-winged blackbirds migrate in a huge wave that reaches from coast to coast. In this particular, story Carl arrived at a pond in Massachusetts at the beginning of March and decided to stay. Other males may have continued to fly as far north as Newfoundland to find a suitable breeding territory.

Upon his arrival, the first thing that Carl needed to do was to secure the best habitat possible and set up a territory. Basically, he was looking for a wet area that was sure to support tall, thick vegetation during the coming summer. This was crucial because the vegetation would provide habitat for the insects that would sustain baby red-wings. Ponds, marshes, wet fields, and moist thickets were all possible choices.

Once Carl picked out a spot, the fighting began. Other male red-wings were just as determined to claim good territories and were willing to fight to maintain their boundaries. They would even displace Carl if he didn't stay alert, so Carl had to put on a show of force. He did this through a combination if color and sound.

In the world of red-winged blackbirds, fighting is done mostly through vocal and visual displays. The familiar "chonk-a-ree" song is really designed to threaten other males while also impressing the ladies. The red-and-yellow shoulder patches are also designed to threaten other males.

Carl spends his days faithfully patrolling the boundaries of his territory and stopping at favored perches where he can sing and show off his bright red feathers. He will sometimes do both at once, puffing up his body feathers, flaring his wings and tail, arching his back, and screaming "chonk-a-ree" at a rival. Occasionally, all of the theatrics are abandoned and a real fight breaks out!

Carl is doing all of this in anticipation of the arrival of female red-winged blackbirds, who are a few weeks behind the males. Female red-wings are very sneaky, secretive birds, and are rarely seen unless you put a little effort into it. They have dark brown feathers with light streaks and though they don't look much like the males, they are just as spunky. Females will fight amongst themselves, but they do so without the pageantry of the males. When females fight, it's all business.

When the females arrive in the next week or so, the males will have well-defined territories marked out. Carl and his neighbors will do their best to show any females that their territories are actually the best ones around, and Carl will surely put on some energetic displays to show how healthy and robust he is.

The females may do some fighting amongst themselves, but eventually a female will choose Carl to be the father of her offspring. Once the choice has been made, however, the most fascinating aspect of the social lives of red-winged blackbirds will begin to unfold. Filled with cheating and deception, the love lives of red-winged blackbirds rival any soap opera.

Almost immediately after Carl hooks up with one female he will set up a "dummy" territory nearby. He will still put a lot of energy into protecting his real territory, but from time to time he will slip off and defend the second territory as well.

Basically, Carl is going to try to get another female to select him, but under the false pretense that he is unattached. If he is successful, this second female will be convinced that he is ready to go, and Carl will mate with her as well. As if that weren't enough, he will then abandon her. He will stick close to his primary female, and even help provide food for his first nest full of little Carls, but the second family will largely be ignored. Instead of helping out with his second family Carl may actually set up a third dummy territory and try to hook up with a third female.

This certainly smacks of the twisted plots of many a daytime soap, and Carl may sound like a real low-life to anyone with strong family values, but before you judge poor Carl too harshly you need to know one additional bit of information.

Although Carl is going to be very clever and deceptive, he may not be quite as smart as we give him credit for. In fact, there exists the very real possibility that each of the females that selects Carl to father their offspring may actually know what is going on. Furthermore, it may in fact be the case that the female red-wings will be using Carl, rather than the other way around.

The real question is this: is Carl a scoundrel or a victim? It turns out that there are many reasons why some female blackbirds are quite content to be single mothers. Carl may play the role of "playboy of the marsh," or "good-time guy," but female red-winged blackbirds are shrewd, calculating, and far from helpless. The lives of red-winged blackbirds are complicated.

In some species of animals there is a definite effort to work together toward a common goal. Males and females work as a team to raise youngsters. This common goal still exists for red-winged blackbirds, but they work solely as individuals. Both sexes are totally self-centered and only come together because sexual reproduction requires it. More astounding, however, may be the fact that both sexes appear to understand this. They have accepted this particular way of life, and spend all of their time trying to get the upper hand.

So now let's look at the world through the eyes of a female red-winged blackbird. Let's call her...Brooke. What kind of challenges does she have to meet? What kind of decisions does she have to make? After this, you may decide that Carl isn't such a bad guy after all.

By the time Brooke arrives on her breeding grounds, in early April, Carl and the rest of the males have already been hard at work setting up territories. Brooke is an older, more experienced female, so she knows how the game is played.

As soon as she arrives she immediately begins a tour of the local marshes and wet meadows. Many males energetically advertise the most favorable territories, while the less attractive areas may only have one or two younger males. Regardless of this, however, Brooke will tour them all.

Since Carl is an older male, experienced and quite dashing, he will undoubtedly have secured himself an impressive territory. Brooke will notice Carl immediately, and for the sake of our story let's just say that Brooke and Carl start to get cozy. It is at this point that the common motive of raising healthy babies will drive Carl and Brooke to very different behaviors, giving us a magnificent chance to explore the differences between males and females.

Red-winged blackbirds are sexually dimorphic, which means that males and females do not look alike. Males are black with red-and-yellow wing patches, while females are a mottled brown. For red-winged blackbirds, these differences are essential to their individual roles in reproduction.

The primary goal of male red-wings is to father as many babies as possible. To do this they need to mate with as many females as possible, so they spend almost all of their time attracting attention to themselves. They are constantly fighting with other males, attracting females, and fighting off predators. Males never incubate eggs, or even help in the building of nests, so they can afford to have bright, flashy feathers.

Females have the same motive as males: produce as many babies as possible. Females, however, can only raise a limited number of babies because they are constrained by the number of eggs they can lay. So their main goal becomes finding the most impressive male to father their offspring. This, by the way, encourages fancy plumage in the males. Females build the nests, incubate the eggs, and feed the babies. The last thing they want to do is attract attention, so their feathers are designed to provide camouflage.

The most experienced females, like Brooke, arrive early in the year and select the healthiest males they can find. Their biggest goal at this point is to become the primary female to the most healthy and robust male available. The males, however, aren't going to be duped. They chase these females quite vigorously in an attempt to assess their health. After all, if they are going to be stuck with a "ball and chain" they should pick the best females possible, right? Watching for this chasing behavior is the best way to find female in early spring.

Once Brooke's position as Carl's primary female is secure, Carl will attempt to attract another female. Brooke, however, will ferociously attack any female that enters Carl's territory. Early in the year, when resources are limited, Brooke has to protect all of Carl's territory if she is to ensure the survival of her first brood.

As soon as she has a clutch of eggs to incubate, however, Carl is pretty much free to do what he wants. He will go in search of another female and if Brooke puts up a fuss Carl may actually attack her. But fear not, Brooke will already be secure. Her babies will hatch first, and Carl will help to feed them. Carl will not assist any of his additional females in this manner.

This is where the secondary females have an important decision to make. Whatever happens, Carl is going to ignore them, but is it better to be the secondary female to an impressive male like Carl, or to be a primary female to a less experienced male? No one really knows how such decisions are made. Secondary females might be younger females who are breeding for the first time, or they may simply be late in arriving on the breeding grounds, but it makes you wonder doesn't it? Maybe these birds are a lot smarter than we give them credit for.

The secondary females may decide that it Carl is simply too impressive to pass up. As a result, Carl may end up with as many as 12 females and many offspring, while many other males may go without any females at all.

Once Brooke's first batch of babies fledges from the nest another aspect of her self-centered behavior kicks in. The only way she can have more offspring is if she abandons her family and starts a new nest. This is where being Carl's main squeeze pays off again.

Since Carl will feed her babies, Brooke can leave them with him while she sets up a new nest nearby. Carl's secondary females do not have this advantage, and as a result they will not have as many babies in one year. Brooke won't even fight with other females at this point because Carl's territory will now provide abundant resources and all of the other females will be busy.

At the end of the year Brooke may have up to three sets of babies, many more than any of Carl's secondary mates, and Carl will have fathered them all. This winning combination of genes will proliferate and the babies will all exhibit the strong qualities of their parents.

So the behavior of red-winged blackbirds actually makes sense. Males and females both have something to offer, but only because it suits their own needs. In addition, their behaviors encourage each other and continue to promote the self-centered lifestyle. Keep this in mind the next time you walk down to a marsh and watch the red-wings.

The Spring Peeper

E ARLY IN THE YEAR, when the nights start to turn balmy and the soft ice cream stands are open again, you will probably discern a slight, but wonderful change in the world. You'll probably notice it on the first evening that you drive with the windows down—a chorus of tiny voices drifting out of ponds, wet fields, and hidden pools in the forest. The question for many people is not so much where the little voices are coming from, but rather who they belong to.

The most common explanation I hear is that the voices belong to crickets. This is a reasonable guess until one realizes that there are no adult crickets in the spring. The only crickets to survive the winter do so in the egg stage, they probably haven't even hatched yet and certainly won't be singing for months to come. So who is making all of this noise? Well, it turns out that all of the ruckus is made by frogs. Specifically, we are hearing the voices of Spring Peepers.

Frogs are common enough so that just about everyone has seen one. On any rainy night in the spring or summer you are apt to see frogs crossing the road, and I hope that you will keep this in

11

mind and try to avoid hitting them. The larger species of aquatic frogs need to stay wet at all times, so they can only travel around when it is raining. Historically it has also been safest for them to travel at night since they cannot easily be found in the dark, but the recent invention of the automobile has screwed things up for them. If you are driving on a rainy night in the spring please keep a lookout for frogs and give them a chance to continue living.

People who work in gardens also tend to see a lot of frogs, but the problem is that whether it is in the road or in a garden, it is usually the same two or three species that are being seen all of the time. These are the pickerel frog, the green frog, and the bullfrog. Pickerel frogs are probably the most commonly seen in your lawn or garden. These frogs are medium sized with golden skin covered with brown spots. When compared to a bullfrog, which is a gigantic, green, and portly, the leopard frog can be described as being "thin." Finally we have the green frog, which lies between the other two in size, but most strongly resembles the bullfrog. When the majority of people think of a frog it is probably the bullfrog that hops into their minds.

Few people, however, are ready to think of frogs as being tiny, but this is exactly what spring peepers are. In fact, spring peepers are so tiny that they can easily sit on your thumbnail and can comfortably perch themselves on top of a quarter. The males are the smallest, measuring a mere three-quarters of an inch in length. A really big male, however, might make it to a full inch! Females are larger and range from an inch to an inch and a quarter. The males may be tiny, but they make up for their small bodies with very loud voices. On a quiet night their songs can travel a half a mile through the woods to drift in through your bedroom window and gently put you to sleep.

Spring peepers are frequently heard but rarely seen. In addition to being tiny, they are also the same color as dead leaves. This is another trait that people are rarely ready for because most people think of frogs as being green.

Green is a fine color for an aquatic species, like a bullfrog, since it will aid in blending in with lily pads, cattail leaves, and other vegetation. For a peeper, however, brown allows them to better blend in with the forest floor, which is generally covered with last year's leaves. So the color of choice for a peeper is brown. The body is a light brown with a dark brown "X" across the back. Both sexes have this mark, and it serves to make them harder to see as they swim among the dead reeds and cattails in the early spring ponds. They are virtually impossible to find in the forest. In fact, if a peeper isn't singing, you will probably never find one.

Spring peepers are members of the Treefrog Family *Hylidae.* Until recently they were considered to be in the treefrog genus *Hyla* and were known specifically as *Hyla pickeringii.* I have a great book titled *The Frog Book,* by Mary C. Dickerson. In it the author refers to the spring peeper as "Pickering's treefrog." Exactly who Pickering was I am not sure, but it is a safe bet that this person was some kind of scientist who studied frogs. Today, scientists have changed the spring peeper's classification and it is now considered to be a Chorus Frog, *Pseudacris crucifer.* I am guessing that the species name *crucifer* in some way refers to the cross on the peeper's back, much like the word "crucifix."

Chorus frogs are still treefrogs, but as a group they are characterized as being small in size, having small toe pads that give them great climbing abilities, and being very hard to find because they gather in vernal pools. Exactly what name the peeper is known by is totally irrelevant to the frogs themselves. We may struggle to correctly classify them, but they have always known who they are.

Unlike green frogs and bullfrogs, spring peepers do not spend the winter buried in the mud at the bottom of ponds and lakes. Instead, they curl up under the leaves on the forest floor and drift into a state of suspended animation. Since they are so close to the surface they warm up quicker than other frogs and are usually the

first to come out of hibernation. Once the warm weather has set-
tled in, and a warm spring rain has fallen, peepers head for marshy
spots such as the margins of quiet ponds, or the temporary pools
of spring meltwater known as "vernal pools." It is there that the
males set about their singing in the hope of attracting a female.

One may wonder why it is that the females are larger than the
males. In mammals, the males tend to be larger because they are generally the ones who do all of the territorial fighting. Large size also
helps when it comes to the battles over individual females. As a result, it is generally the largest males that have the most reproductive success, so their sons tend to be larger and their daughters tend
to mate with larger males.

That may be fine for mammals, but reptiles and amphibians
have an entirely different approach to life. Female amphibians
rarely carry their young internally, and instead lay masses of eggs
in a body of water. Since sperm cells are small even the smallest
male frogs can produce millions of them. Eggs, on the other
hand, are large enough to quickly fill a female's body. So, it is
the production of eggs that represents the only limiting factor
for a female frog's reproductive capacity. Logically, a larger body
can hold more eggs, so the larger females have an advantage.

Female peepers are still not very large, so they never lay
that many eggs. The eggs themselves are tiny and resemble the
small seeds of plants. They may be laid singly on the leaves at
the bottom of pools, but sometimes they are laid in small masses
on twigs. A protective covering resembling Jell-O surrounds each
egg. Since vernal pools are temporary by nature, speed is of the
essence and the young peepers develop quickly. The eggs hatch
12 days after they are laid, and the small *pollywogs* quickly develop into adults. Of all of the life stages, the pollywogs are probably the easiest to observe if you sit next to a woodland pool
and watch carefully.

So once the weather starts to warm up again I hope that all of you parents of little children will consider grabbing a flashlight and taking your little ones for a frog hunt. Children seem to have an affinity for frogs, although it can often be mixed with a little hesitant respect for something that is so "slimy." In fact, frogs aren't really slimy at all. Slippery would be a better term, and this may serve to ease some nerves.

Trying to find a peeper can be a lot of fun as long as you don't ever expect to see one. It often takes me an hour or more to catch a peeper and I know what I am doing. It might only take ten minutes to narrow my search down to a square foot of marsh grass, but finding the tiny beasts is never easy. They blend in, they climb up above the water, and they stop singing if you move.

Just remember that peepers are very tiny, rather delicate, and excited children have a tendency to squeeze. Also, you should always dunk your hands in water before picking up a peeper. Children seem to love the game of hide and seek though, so it is worth it.

Skunk Cabbage

A T ABOUT THE SAME TIME that the peepers start to fill the evenings with their wonderful little voices there comes another sure sign of spring. A few of the resident birds might begin to sing, and perhaps some early migrants will appear, but the sign I speak of will be popping up out of the ground. I'm talking about flowers.

Now, we can't really count the cultivated bulbs among the signs of spring because, well, they're cultivated. When I say the flowers are blooming I am speaking of the wildflowers. Early in the spring, however, there is only one flower that could be in bloom, and it may come as something of a surprise to you. This is a flower not often thought of, although the plant itself is relatively well known. Can you guess? It's the skunk cabbage.

This plant is quite common in open swamps and marshes, in wet woodlands, and along streams. Its bright green leaves lend a certain tropical quality to the understory of our northern temperate forests, and they give off a decidedly "skunky" odor when crushed. Thus, we get the source of the name skunk, but I have no idea why anyone thought this plant resembled a cabbage.

16

The leaves can be up to 2 feet long and 1 foot wide and each grows directly out of the ground. That famous ingester of wild plants, Euell Gibbons, actually tried to eat skunk cabbage leaves on one occasion, and reported that the young shoots tasted as bad as they smelled. There was also a strong burning in the mouth and throat that made the entire experience most unpleasant. He finally managed to find a method of preparing this unlikely food, which involved cutting the shoots into thin slices and drying them for 10 months. When crushed, mixed 1:1 with wheat flour, and made into pancakes the dried leaves tasted okay. It turns out that the drying process is the only way to destroy the effects of the calcium oxalate crystals that produce the burning reaction of fresh leaves, but why would you bother? Gibbons certainly didn't know.

The plant may be familiar to some, but its flowers may not be terribly well known. This is probably due to a combination of three of the flower's characteristics. First, while they are technically flowers, you might not know this by looking at them. The skunk cabbage is a member of the *Arum* Family, which has some 2,000 members found worldwide. This family has some very well known members, and some classic flowers, but they do not conform to the model of a flower which may reside in your head. For instance, there are no actual petals and the remaining sexual elements of the flowers are very tiny and crowded onto a fleshy spike called a *spadix* which resembles an ear of corn.

The spadix is surrounded, and in the case of the skunk cabbage —enclosed, by a fleshy and often showy *spathe*. The spathe can be any color. In the case of the skunk cabbage it varies from a mottled green to the deep red of an eggplant. Its most famous cousin has a white spathe that looks like a single beautiful petal. One more hint and then you have to guess at the identity of this famous cousin. Ready? Unlike the skunk cabbage, this famous flower is located on the end of a long, thin, green stem. Have you got it? You won't believe this.

The identity of the mystery cousin is the cala lily! Here in the Northeast we have the North American version, the wild cala, which is similar but not as elegant as the tropical cala lily. Another well-known member of the *Arum* Family is the Jack-in-the-pulpit, which is also very common in our area.

The second characteristic that may be keeping skunk cabbage flowers out of the limelight is the fact that they can start blooming as early as February. Finally, the skunk cabbage is found in wet areas, which are generally avoided in the spring, and so the flowers may pass unnoticed. They are definitely worth finding, however, because they are quite attractive. So the next time you are looking for something to do on a sunny morning in March, why not put on some good waterproof boots and head out to find the first flowers of the year? You can start by looking next to that stream you pass by on your way to work. Remember to bring a camera, because skunk cabbage flowers can be beautiful.

Look for an area that is low and quite wet. Streams with steep banks won't be of much help, but the flat areas that may be flooded during the peak of the spring runoff might prove to be fruitful. The skunk cabbage flower is about as big as your fist and vaguely pear-shaped. The flower forces its way through the wet leaves on the forest floor, and may be partially covered by them, so don't be afraid to poke around a little.

This flower blooms so early in the year that it may even force its way up through snow. Fear not for the flower of the skunk cabbage though, for it is about as delicate as its scent is sweet. Because of its rapid growth, the heat generated from cellular respiration is actually sufficient to melt snow. Even on cold days the microclimate inside the hollow of the spathe can actually be a pleasant 72° F. This is of particular importance because there are a precious few pollinating insects that are active so early in the year.

Among those insects that emerge early in the spring are carrion flies, and they provide us with the ultimate explanation for the skunk cabbage's skunky smell. Carrion flies are attracted to the fetid odor of rotting meat, so skunk cabbage leaves and flowers produce a nasty, rotten smell in an attempt to lure the flies to act as pollinators. The heat-producing character of the flowers further encourages the flies to visit by providing them with a nice warm shelter from the cold.

On some days skunk cabbages may be the only reason that the flies can get around at all. They may zip into one flower and spend a while warming up before moving on to the next flower. Bees have also been known to do this, and on days when the temperature falls below 65° F they will be unable to fly at all unless they are able to find an external source of heat. On such days, skunk cabbage flowers act like little saunas and allow flies and bees alike to remain active.

On a day when the last of the snow has melted from the forest floor, look for the strange but beautiful flowers of skunk cabbages as they push themselves out of the ground. You may find that regardless of their odor, you will wish that you were small enough to crawl inside where it is nice and warm.

Shrews

THERE ARE MANY PARTS of the world that we humans are simply not privy to. Because we are large, terrestrial mammals we generally don't get a chance to see what is happening under water, up in the sky, or even in the treetops. These are places we simply aren't designed to be. We are also designed for the daylight hours, so we miss out on most of what happens at night. But even during the day there are things that happen at ground level which most of us never see.

This is a byproduct of the way our bodies have been shaped by evolution. We walk on two feet instead of the customary four, and as a result we are very tall. Our eyes and ears are perched atop our shoulders some 5–6 feet of the ground, and we rarely get down on all fours.

So there is a lot that goes on, literally under our noses, that we rarely notice because our eyes and ears are too far away from the ground and our attention is elsewhere. Only through constant practice can we relearn those skills of observation that allow us to detect the hidden world right beneath our feet. Other times we must rely on dumb luck.

As a wildlife biologist and naturalist, I have spent many years teaching myself how to be observant. My ears are always straining to hear faint sounds, my eyes are always searching for slight movements or patches of color that are out of place, and I am even getting to be pretty good at detecting and identifying faint odors.

There is also a trick that I will share with you. When you are in the woods you should slow down and watch where you put your feet. If you see something interesting, get down and take a good long look at it up close. Then, before you get up again, look around you. There may be other things of interest that you hadn't noticed while you were standing.

One day, while out for a walk in the woods looking for flowers, I decided to head off into the forest to see what I might have missed on previous hikes. A flower caught my eye so I got down on all fours to get a better look at it, and while I was down there I saw something quite out of the ordinary. It was an owl pellet, and protruding out of one of its sides was a tiny skull.

I suspect that at this point at least some of you are thinking, "an owl what?" An owl pellet is a byproduct of digestion. Hair and bones, which are too tough to digest, are collected in the stomach, molded into a pellet, and regurgitated after the rest of the body has been dissolved.

As gruesome as this may sound, the discovery of an owl pellet is actually something that will excite most naturalists because the bones can often be identified. Most small mammals are difficult for humans to find, but owls are expert small mammal detectors. Often, owl pellets provide the only direct evidence that certain animals are in a given area.

So how about the owl pellet I found? What did it tell me about the forest I was exploring? Fortunately, the skull was sticking out of the pellet nose-first and I immediately knew that it was the skull of a shrew. All I had to do was look at the teeth.

Shrews are small animals that bear a superficial resemblance to mice. Both are small, and both are mammals, but this is where the similarities stop. Mice are rodents. Most rodents are primarily vegetarians and their teeth have been shaped by this lifestyle. They have very large incisors for chopping their food, and well-developed molars for grinding their food, but they have no canine teeth.

Shrews, on the other hand, are predators. They hunt and kill other animals, and have a full compliment of teeth to help them do it. Predators also have knife-like molars that are designed for slicing rather than grinding. The teeth in the skull were definitely those of a predator, but there are other small predatory animals which owls also eat. Moles, like shrews, make a living by hunting and killing other animals, and their teeth are very similar to those of shrews. There is, however, one key characteristic that differentiates the teeth of shrews from those of any other small mammal— color.

For some reason, the tips of shrew teeth are usually chestnut in color. This coloring was clearly visible on the teeth in the owl pellet, so there was absolutely no doubt that the skull belonged to a shrew.

There are many shrews that live in North America, but there are only a few that can be found in Massachusetts. One of them, the short-tailed shrew *(Blarnia brevicauda)* also happens to be the largest North American shrew. Based on the size of the skull in the owl pellet, I believe that it once belonged to a short-tailed shrew.

Weighing in at an impressive one ounce, and measuring up to 5 inches in length, the short-tailed shrew is a ferocious killer. It attacks snails, slugs, earthworms, beetles, and various other invertebrates with savage bites to the head, paralyzing them almost instantly with venomous saliva. Shrews can even capture mice in this fashion, but the mice are generally not dead when the shrews start eating them.

This ferocity is for good reason, however. Shrews are the mammalian equivalents to hummingbirds. The smallest mammal on Earth is a shrew, and being tiny comes at a high price. Like hummingbirds, shrews have an extremely fast metabolism. They must constantly eat to keep warm, and without food, they could starve to death in a matter of hours. A short-tailed shrew must eat its own bodyweight every day, and this means that the shrew must be active day and night.

Shrews do take the time to reproduce, but not too much. Shrew encounters tend to be somewhat tense, since hunting territory is so valuable. When two shrews of the same sex meet there is often a terrible fight, but members of a mated pair will tolerate one another and maintain a relationship of sorts.

When born, shrews are tiny, pink, and helpless babies who are completely reliant on their mothers for food and protection. Baby shrews also exhibit a unique defense mechanism when danger is near. Each baby shrew will grasp the tail of its closest sibling with its mouth. The baby at the head of this chain then grabs on to Mom's tail, and off they go. I have never seen this, but I suspect that the little shrew train is actually kind of cute.

Shrews live brief, action packed lives. A shrew that dies of old age at two years in not necessarily too old to keep going, but constant chewing on insect exoskeletons wears their teeth down to the point where they can no longer eat. Basically, they end up starving to death.

Most shrews probably live for no more than a few months before they are caught by snakes, owls, and other predators. Their high level of activity, however, probably makes their lives seem twice as long. Yet, as active as shrews are they are seldom seen by humans. Shrews spend a lot of time in tunnels just below the surface of the forest floor where they are most likely to find their next meal. They are also very fast, but this is not sufficient defense against owls.

The next time you go out into the woods take a careful look around. If you are lucky, you may actually find an owl pellet someday, and if you find chestnut stains on the tips of any teeth then you will know that there are some amazing little animals are living their amazing little lives right near you.

The Eastern Phoebe

A T ABOUT SEVEN INCHES in length phoebes are a bit on the small side. Their coloration is also a bit on the subdued side—being all grays and browns—but don't be fooled: Phoebes are more than capable of compensating for their diminutive size and quiet colors with a great big personality!

The name "Pheobe" (pronounced fEE-bEE) is nothing more than a simple human imitation of a relatively simple bird song. Not the clear, sweet notes of a chickadee's song (also known as a phoebe song), the phoebe's buzzy voice produces a two-note song that is sassy and emphatic. I've been waiting to use the word "emphatic" for months!

The phoebe in my neighborhood *(Saynoris phoebe)* is not the only one that occurs in the United States. It is, however, the only phoebe which occurs in the eastern U.S., so it has been assigned the mercifully simple common name, "eastern phoebe." Fans of the etymology of words will enjoy the story behind the phoebe's genus name.

Way back in the good old days, long before there were 50 United States, there were parts of the American west that had yet to be explored by European colonists. Lewis and Clark went on a famous adventure in 1805, but they didn't see everything.

Many expeditions headed into the western part of the continent, and in 1814 a scientist named Thomas Say accompanied Major Stephen H. Long on an expedition into the Rocky Mountains. Say's role was that of a naturalist and he prepared a report on the birds that he encountered, one of which was a phoebe.

Well, it turns out that Say was also a famous entomologist (bug guy) and he impressed a lot of people. So, to commemorate him and his contributions to the study of birds on the Rocky Mountain expedition, the genus for phoebes was named in his honor. The word *Sayornis* is a blending of Say's name and the Greek word, *ornis* meaning, "bird." Phoebes are Say's birds.

The phoebe that Say encountered in the Rockies was also named in his honor, and is known as Say's phoebe *(Sayornis saya)*. In the extreme southwestern United States there is the Black phoebe *(Sayornis nigricans)*, and in the east we have the eastern phoebe. Oddly enough, the eastern phoebe's scientific name *(Sayornis phoebe)* is the one that best compliments the common name of the Say's phoebe. Go figure.

So what can I tell you about the eastern phoebe? For starters you should probably know that phoebes are members of a group of birds known as "flycatchers." They are bright-eyed and zippy little birds that make a living by sitting on exposed perches, waiting for flying insects to pass by, and catching them. This particular foraging strategy is known as *hawking*.

Phoebes belong to a sub-grouping of flycatchers known as the "tyrant flycatchers," a collection of birds known for their energy and their generally impudent approach to life. Every phoebe I have ever seen has given me the impression that it was perturbed about one thing or another, and thinking about it now just makes me laugh.

I'm laughing because I also know how sweet these birds can actually be. As a licensed wildlife rehabilitator, I have raised many nests of phoebes, and I have learned something of them. They are definitely spunky, but it is more a result of being constantly on the lookout for fast and elusive prey rather than any anger or malice. Imagine a little bird which has just had six cups of coffee and you will be close to the energy level of a phoebe.

If you want to find a phoebe you can start by finding yourself a horse. Phoebes like flies, horses attract flies, so phoebes like horses too. In fact, phoebes will even incorporate horsehair into their nests if they live near a farm.

Oh yes, the nests. Phoebe nests are made of mud and plant fibers and are lined with soft plant downs, feathers, and hair. Construction of a phoebe nest takes one to two weeks because phoebes can only transport mud one beak-full at a time. The male does not help.

If you ever find a phoebe's nest, you will also notice that the nest is covered with moss, an interesting artifact of phoebe history. In a natural setting, empty of any buildings, phoebes might nest in trees or in niches in cliffs. In such locations camouflage is useful, so phoebes decorate their nests with moss.

These days, however, phoebes have abandoned their old nest sites for new ones. Phoebes love to nest in the eaves of buildings, or in the rafters of barns. I have even found phoebe nests that were built under decks. I guess phoebes just like the cozy feeling of a roof over their heads.

The standard phoebe clutch contains 4-5 white eggs. The babies that hatch out of the eggs start out like most any songbird; naked, blind, and helpless, but they grow very quickly on a diet of flying insects. Little phoebes also happen to be adorable.

Their feathers match the pattern of the adults, but their breast feathers have a lemony tint to them rather than being white. Young phoebes also have amazingly gentle little voices too, and they sound almost like crickets. When they get hungry their voices become harsh and urgent, but once they have eaten they revert back to their little cricket calls, closing their eyes, going to sleep, and quietly cricketing to themselves.

Phoebe fledglings are also a great deal of fun because they are small, fast, and quite inquisitive. They see everything and they are not at all shy about stealing food out of your hand. I understand that this is because they have to learn the art of hawking, but it is always a surprise when I walk outside and am instantly surrounded by a swarm of hungry phoebes that I have raised, each trying to take food I haven't even offered yet. Once they catch their first bugs, however, they have no further use for humans. The only way to distinguish them from adults is to note the darker feathers on the upper breast.

Before they disappear into the wild it is interesting to watch a very distinct phoebe characteristic develop over time. For some reason, which escapes me completely, eastern phoebes have a habit of bobbing their tails up and down. Tiny phoebes don't do this too much, but as their tails begin to grow the bobbing starts. The longer their tails get, the more they bob them until their tails are almost constantly in motion. Any little gray-and-white bird that is bobbing its tail is an eastern phoebe.

This is important to know because there is another flycatcher, known as an eastern wood pee-wee, which looks almost exactly like an eastern phoebe. From a distance they are almost indistinguishable, except for that one little trait on the part of phoebes.

During the winter phoebes move as far south as Mexico in search of live, flying insects. When the warm weather returns, so so do the phoebes. So the next time you are out for a walk, particularly in the morning, listen for the excited little two-note call of the eastern phoebe.

Farms and marshes are great places to look for them. Should you locate a phoebe, take the time to watch it for a while. You'll be impressed with its flying skills and amused by its constant tail bobbing and occasional exclamation of "Fee-bee!" as if it is reminding the entire world that a little tyrant is on the scene.

Spring Wildflowers

HAVE YOU EVER looked at something, turned around for just a minute, looked back, and found that things had changed on you? Spring has a way of doing these things to all of us because plants can grow so quickly. One minute the trees in the back yard are bare and then suddenly they have leaves. One minute the field down the road is covered with dead brown grass and the next it has changed to a vibrant green. You have to pay attention or you just might miss something.

This is certainly true when it comes to the wildflowers. Sometimes you have to keep an eye out for a little splash of color here or there, and other times you can be completely stupefied by the sheer number of flowers in a meadow. You never really know what you are going to find around the next corner so you should always be ready and willing to stop and take a look.

I thought I might create a day of flower finding for you. Anyone reading this article could easily recreate some of it by going out and taking a walk. So are you ready? Pay attention so I don't have to write all of this again, okay? Here we go:

It's Sunday morning, the sun is shining and you get out of bed at 5:30 a.m. You quickly throw on some old jeans and a sweatshirt, grab a quick glass of OJ, and in just 7 minutes you're ready to...Wait a minute, wait a minute, hold on, *whoa!* For a minute there I forgot that I was writing a flower-watching story and I started with an introduction to a bird watching story. Sorry, everyone. There is no need to get up early, or even do anything out of the ordinary this morning. That's the great thing about wildflowers. So let me start again.

It's Sunday morning, it's. . . 8:30 a.m., and you don't really care what it is doing outside. It's your day off. You get out of bed and throw on some old. . . slippers, grab a cup of something warm to drink, and in just 20 minutes you're ready to. . . go get the morning paper. It isn't raining or anything, and as you walk down the driveway you notice a couple of spots of color in the lawn.

The dandelions are easy to spot. Normally you would make a mental note to find a way to get rid of them, but you are in a really good mood. So instead of cursing them you bend down to look at one. It actually is a very beautiful flower isn't it? As you look closer you notice that the dandelion flower isn't just one flower, but a collection of many tiny flowers in an *inflorescence.* Then you recall something you learned about flowers in Junior High. Something about stanems, stymes, or stamens? Stamens, that's right. Didn't they also have something to do with guns?

You take a sip of your drink, sit down in the grass, close your eyes, and begin to remember. Flowers generally have four main parts. The *sepals* are what cover the flower when it is still in the bud stage. As soon as the flower blooms they tend to just curl up and roll out of the way. The *petals* are usually bright colors and they are designed to give birds and insects a bright target. Then you get to the important parts, the *stamens* and *pistils.*

The *stamens* are the male parts of the flowers and are composed of a long *filament* with an *anther* at the top. The anther is where the pollen is produced and each grain of pollen contains sperm cells. The filament holds the anthers up so the pollen can be out in the open. The *pistils* (not pistols) are the female portions of flowers. They are composed of *ovaries,* a *style,* and a *stigma.* The ovaries hold the egg cells, the style is basically the same as a filament, and the stigma rests upon the top of the style and has a sticky surface to capture pollen.

You smile to yourself and think that there is no reason to attach a stigma to a bad smelling flower because it still has style. Yikes, what was in that drink?

Shaken from your memories, your eyes pop open, you get up and look around real quick to make sure no one saw you taking your trip down memory lane, and you head for the mailbox. You think, "the morning paper should be here by now," but before you get that far you notice some other flowers in the lawn. There are blue and white violets, those are pretty easy, but there is another one you aren't too sure about. You grab the paper, pick one of these mystery flowers, and head for the kitchen.

Once inside you go and grab your flower guide (everyone should have one) and you start the process of identification. Let's see...it has purple flowers, the main stem is square instead of round, and the leaves are very small with scalloped edges. The book says it is a flower called Jill-over-the-ground, or ground-ivy. It's pretty enough but, ah, it's an alien. You want to find the native wildflowers.

So, you decide to head out for a walk in the woods. It could be a state park, a state forest, or just the conservation area in your neighborhood. A quick drive and you're there (wherever there may be), and you're on the trail for a nice walk. Already you are seeing flowers. There is a large, dark-red flower with only three petals over there to the right. That's an easy one to start with, it is the purple trillium. This is one of the most attractive wild-flowers of the spring, and it is one of the most common of the eastern trilliums. Don't try to smell it though, because it produces the smell of rotten meat.

You see, instead of depending on bees for pollination, the trillium attracts carrion flies, so rotting meat is the perfume of choice. In the old days, herbalists believed that plants could be used to cure things which they resembled. In the case of the purple trillium, which has a rotten smell, the ailment it was thought to cure was gangrene.

If you walk past a swampy spot you will likely catch sight of a beautiful plant covered with bright yellow flowers. These usually grow in shallow running water and they look like a potted plant that has been set into a stream. This is the marsh marigold. Also known as cowslip, this flower belongs to the buttercup family. This is another of the most showy and attractive wildflowers in our area, and they can often be seen from your car as you drive past marshy areas.

If you wander past an old abandoned homestead in the forest, you might come upon a carpet of periwinkles. These lavender flowers, also known as myrtle, have five petals with angled ends that resemble airplane propellers. You consult the flower book and notice that they were actually introduced, but are now growing wild. Make a note of this spot, however, because there might be some wild daylilies there later in the season.

As you continue your walk you come upon an odd looking red and yellow flower in a rocky area. The flowers "look" down at the ground, and appear to be composed of tubular, red petals with very long pistils and stamens. A quick look in the flower book confirms your suspicions; this is wild columbine. A particular favorite of ruby-throated hummingbirds, this is a nectar producing flower that also attracts many species of butterflies.

Then you come upon two very odd looking plants by the side of a field. One is not even green, but rather a pinkish-tan. It has what appears to be a cone-shaped...thing...at the top of the stem. It actually reminds you of asparagus. Look as you may, however, you cannot find it in your flower book. Well don't worry, it isn't in any of my flower books either. It isn't a flower. To find this one you would need to get a book on ferns.

This is the field horsetail—the most common of the many species of horsetails—and it can be found growing in almost any soil. They will grow on the sides of railroad tracks, slag heaps, and vacant lots, but you can also find them in fields and wooded areas that get some sunlight. They are still rather beautiful, so I thought you might like to know what they are.

The other odd looking flower is called the Jack-in-the-pulpit. It resembles a cala lily, but the "hood" of the flower actually forms something of a roof over the rest of the long, fluted flower. The name is said to have come from the fact that the yellowish repro-ductive portion of the plant, also called the *spadix,* resembles a preacher standing in a pulpit. It's a bit of a stretch, but the flower is definitely worth looking for. Try to remember where you find one because if you return later in the year you will find that an ear of crimson-colored berries has replaced the flower.

Another beautiful flower is the trout lily. This is an easy one to identify because the leaves grow directly out of the ground and are green mottled with brown. The flowers themselves are bright yellow with six petals. The entire plant stands about ten inches off the ground and the flowers "look" down, but if you are gentle you can bend them upward for a better look. These are definitely worth finding!

The further you walk, and the more often you walk, the more you will see. There are hundreds of wildflowers that bloom during the spring, summer, and fall, and every day there will be something new. Be careful though, because they won't last forever. Most wild-flowers only bloom for short periods of time. The flowers that re-place them will be magnificent, however, so don't think that there is nothing to see.

There are wild bleeding hearts, Dutchman's breeches, May ap-ples, Dutchman's pipe, hawkweed, devil's bit, and a tall flowering shrub called pinxter flower. These pinxters are beautiful to look at and have a very nice perfume to them as well! You can identify these flowers with the help of a *Peterson's Wildflower Guide,* an Audubon Society *Field Guide to North American Wildflowers,* or the *Newcomb's Wildflower Guide.* These books generally cost between $14 and $20 and can be found at your local bookstore or nature store. You can even try the library.

Whatever you do just make sure you go for a walk. The world is just too nice a place to ignore, and wildflowers are something that people of every age can enjoy. Many of your local state forests and parks should give guided wildflower walks every weekend too. So grab a book, head for a hike, and look for some flowers. Just re-member that you can't wear you slippers in the woods and you'll be just fine.

The Garter Snake

EVERY SPRING, as temperatures start to rise, humans get more active. They emerge from their dens and start cleaning garages, firing up barbecues, and working in gardens. This may seem to be a perfectly innocent group of activities, but they are not always "Nature Friendly." As humans get outside more they are more likely to encounter the animals that live around their homes, and these encounters are not always good news for the animals.

Take, for instance, snakes. Most snakes are rarely seen by people and do nothing at all to bother us. In fact, many species are valuable to farmers because they prey upon rats and mice. To further expound on the benefits of snakes I should also mention that these fascinating animals are valuable assets to any ecosystem, and in most cases they are extraordinary beautiful. Yet, despite all of this, humans almost universally loathe snakes.

Being a human myself, I was out raking the lawn the other day and I saw a garter snake slipping through the grass in an attempt to avoid being raked. Did I scream? Did I run and get a shovel? No! Instead, I admired the beauty of the snake's seemingly effortless movements and I felt good knowing there was a snake in my yard. My world had just become a little more interesting.

Unfortunately, snakes do not always fare so well. I have heard many stories of snakes found in yards and far too many of these stories ended in, "So I killed it." Well, I happen to like snakes and I am greatly saddened every time I hear that particular ending. So, in an effort to save as many of these wonderful animals as possible, I am going to try to present snakes in the proper light.

Snakes are a wildly successful group of reptiles. They can be found on all but one of Earth's continents. Can you guess which continent has no snakes? The answer is Antarctica. It simply isn't a place that many things can live, particularly cold-blooded terrestrial things like snakes. Snakes do inhabit every other continent, however, starting above the Arctic Circle and extending almost to the tip of Argentina.

There are roughly 2,700 species of snakes known to exist on our planet. They can be found from below sea level to an altitude of 16,000 feet in the Himalayan Mountains, and within this range they exploit the entire spectrum of habitats. There are sea snakes, which never even come up on land, and snakes of the deserts, prairies, forests, and steppes. Some are terrestrial while others are arboreal; some are gigantic while others are tiny. Snakes are everywhere and they play an important role in every ecosystem they inhabit.

The problem that snakes face is the simple fact that they are a little unsettling at first glance. They have no eyelids, so they perpetually stare out at the world. They have no limbs, yet they can move very quickly over land or through the water. Snakes are also cold blooded so they enjoy basking in the sun whenever they can. Coming upon a perfectly motionless snake that suddenly comes to life and moves away at high speed can be both startling and spooky.

Then, of course, there is the fact that a small percentage of snakes are venomous. This is definitely a drawback, but you have to remember that venomous snakes are rare. Roughly 80% (2,160 species) of the world's snakes belong to one family: the *Colubridae*. These snakes are not venomous at all and pose no threat to humans. North America has 115 species of snakes, and my home state of Massachusetts has only 14. Twelve of them (85%) belong to the harmless *Colubridae* Family.

Of these snakes, the most commonly seen would have to be the garter snake — the very same species that I saw in my lawn. The most widely distributed snake in all of the United States, its range extends from Quebec to Florida, west to California and British Columbia. The only places where garter snakes cannot be found are in the arid southwest and the driest of the Great Plains.

As a result of this huge range, the garter snake *(Thamnophis sirtalis)* is currently in the middle of speciation — a process by which one species of animal becomes two or more separate species. This is made possible by the fact that garter snakes in California have no idea what the garter snakes in Massachusetts are up to. They never encounter one another and never reproduce with one another, allowing small differences in appearance to become bigger.

The standard model for the garter snake is as follows: Small head, large eyes, an average maximum size of no more than 24 inches in length, and a slender body that is either black or dark-brown and marked with 3 parallel yellow stripes running the length of the body. The scales of the belly are yellow.

Here in the eastern US, however, there are a few "Eastern" garter snakes that are different in appearance. The black coloration may be broken with lighter patches of greenish scales that give the snake a checkered appearance. In Oregon, the "Red-spotted" garter snake has distinct red scales and black bands that extend onto the belly. Way down in Florida there is even a "Blue-striped" garter snake that has 3 parallel blue stripes instead of the standard yellow. All are garter snakes, and can reproduce with one another, but given enough time they may become so different that they become distinct species unto themselves.

Wherever you may be, you can expect to run across a garter snake just about anywhere. I have encountered them in dry forests, on top of mountains, and in rocky areas, but their favorite habitat is found in wet fields and around ponds. Garter snakes feed on frogs, toads, salamanders and insects — all of which can be found in wet places.

Garter snakes can occasionally attain a length of 4 feet, at which point they are able to prey on larger animals such as mice and small fish. I have seen many garter snakes in the wild, but I have never seen one that was much over two feet long. Even though they are relatively small, however, they can put on a show of being fierce.

I clearly remember the day I was hiking in the Holyoke Range State Park when I came upon a beautiful garter snake sunning itself on top of a mountain. It was around two feet long, and attempted to get away from me, but I didn't even notice it until it decided to turn and stand its ground. To do this the snake curled itself into the classic pose of a rattlesnake ready to strike. When I decided to get down on the ground and get a closer look at the snake it even lashed out and tried to strike, but I wasn't fooled. Even the hardest bite from a garter snake is nothing compared to the bite of an angry chickadee. To the snake, however, this was a last-chance act of desperation — the only attack it was capable of.

Summer is the breeding season for garter snakes. From June to August the largest breeding females may give birth to as many as 85 live young. Needless to say, these baby snakes are very tiny, and very cute. They make their living by eating very small animals, such as crickets and earth worms, and must do a great deal of growing before they can tackle frogs.

So, keeping all of this in mind, don't freak out the next time you see a snake. Instead, try looking at it for a minute before you do anything else. If you are lucky, the snake will freeze in place, hoping that you don't see it, and affording you the opportunity to look at the patterns on its scales. Then find a snake book and try to look it up. Odds are you will have found a new neighbor that will make your yard a richer and more interesting place.

SUMMER

Canoeing

STARTING IN MY CHILDHOOD, and then continuing on into my adult life as a wildlife biologist, naturalist, and photographer, canoes have played an important role on my life. I have canoed lakes in the Adirondacks and explored small rivers in the White Mountain National Forest and the Pine Barrens of New Jersey. I have traveled larger rivers like the Connecticut and the Mississippi, followed the Intercoastal Waterways of Maryland and Virginia, and lost myself in the enormity of the flooded bottomland hardwood forests of the White River National Wildlife Refuge in Arkansas.

Then there were times when I just floated in the middle of a lake on a warm summer night and listened to owls while I watched for satellites passing through the constellations.

Every trip was a memorable one, and each allowed me to get closer to nature. I could arrive quietly, ease back against a comfortable cushion and watch the world go by, and then leave without having any impact on the events around me.

BOTH A TOOL AND A TOY

The design of the boat is the key. Canoes are long, slender, and have rounded bottoms that allow them to move through the water with a minimum of resistance. While a canoe can take you almost anywhere, their golden element is shallow, weedy water. Again, their design is the key. Their shape allows them to draw very little water and their passengers provide propulsion so there is a minimum of drag and no extra weight.

Any kind of watercraft can be used in deep, open water, but only a canoe can get you into a quiet cove where sunfish nest in the shallows. Only a canoe is quiet enough to ease up on a family of geese, or gently explore the shoreline of a pond looking for the blossoms of water lilies and pickerelweed.

Let's not forget the versatility of a canoe, however. In addition to shallow water, they can take you down a raging river, help you cross a great lake, and even patrol estuaries and calm coastal waters. They can go just about anywhere, carry just about anything, and the only fuel they require is a picnic lunch. In an age of engines and oil, canoes give us a chance to become a part of nature again, even if it's just for a little while.

As a naturalist and scientist, it is this quality of canoes that I find so appealing. These boats allow humans to blend into the environment while also giving us access to habitats that we normally couldn't experience. But the real beauty of canoes is the fact that anyone can get one.

For instance, I have a canoe that I picked up at a yard sale for $25. It may not be the canoe of my dreams, but until I can save enough money to buy the one I really want, the $25 model does just fine. I just have to remind myself that materials and appearance are not the important things in a canoe. All it needs to do it float and be maneuverable.

As long as you have these two characteristics, you can head out into any of our local lakes, ponds, or rivers and get up close and personal with nature. The important thing to do is practice steering and paddling so that you can do everything you need to with a minimum of effort. Once this is accomplished you can blend right in.

TRICKS OF THE TRADE

Nature is always more interesting when you know what you're looking at. Even more exciting is a quest for something that you know about but have never seen before. So in an attempt to make your next canoe trip more interesting here are some things to look for.

The edges of lakes, ponds, and rivers are where most of the action can be found. The transition zone from terrestrial to aquatic habitats is one if the most appealing ecotones in our environment. Because it also happens to be an extremely diverse and fertile zone for plants and insects, the larger vertebrates like fish and birds are drawn to it as well.

For instance, have you ever been paddling through the shallows of a quiet lake and found large, sandy depressions in the soft, mucky bottom? Usually they look like bomb craters and are about the size of a large pizza. Well believe it or not, these structures are actually fish nests.

Yes you heard me correctly, I said fish nests. Shallow water is sunny and warm, and the edges of ponds and lakes are the best places to find sand and gravel. I just so happens that this is exactly what a sunfish is looking for when it comes time to lay eggs.

The nest is actually excavated by a male. His goal is to move away all of the muck and debris until only clean gravel remains. This is accomplished with powerful beatings of the tail while the fish is on its side. When complete, the female will lay her eggs and the male immediately fertilizes them.

Amazingly, the male will then stay with the nest and protect the eggs from predators. Guard duty is not all that is in store for the male, however, for the eggs need some special attention too. The adult fish also fans fresh water over the eggs so that the developing young have an adequate supply of oxygen. Once the little fish hatch they are on their own, but until that time their dear old dad watches over them.

Another animal that is frequently asked about is that funny little bird that hangs around muddy areas. This is a small bird with a brown head and back and a white, speckled belly. What catches people's attention is the little dance this bird does. A couple steps forward, a bob up and down, a step backward, a bob, a sprint forward, a bob...you get the idea.

Well the mystery is finally over! This bird is the spotted sandpiper. People normally think of sandpipers as "ocean birds," but this is simply because people see them at the ocean when people go to the ocean. If you were to follow one of these birds for a month, however, you would quickly discover that they are not strictly ocean birds. Most sandpipers do in fact travel through coastal areas during their migrations, and the majority of them spend the winter months on tropical beaches, but most of them breed in fresh water marshes above the Arctic Circle.

The spotted sandpiper's breeding range is much larger than those of other shorebirds and extends from the Labrador Sea above Newfoundland, Hudson Bay above Ontario, and the Bering Sea on the Alaskan coast, down to California, Texas, and North Carolina. They are quite common on lakes and other bodies of quiet water with muddy shores. The bobbing dance is a sure give-away that you are looking at a spotted sandpiper.

Water lilies will also catch a lot of attention and this is the time to find them all in bloom. The astute observer will quickly notice, however, that there are three kinds of "lily pads", but only two flowers. Fear not, the answer is simple. There are indeed three kinds of flowers, but one doesn't really look like a flower.

The first of the really nice flowers is that of the fragrant water lily. This is probably the lily that everyone thinks of when they hear the name "water lily." The flower is composed of layer upon layer of tapered white petals that open to reveal a golden-yellow center. As its name suggests, the flower has a wonderful fragrance.

These lilies do not grow everywhere and the blossoms do close up during the evening. If you are unable to locate a flower you should look for the round pads of the fragrant water lily. These are about the size of a saucer and have what looks like a slice of pizza missing. Just imagine a green "PacMan" and you'll have the correct search image in your head.

As you look for the fragrant water lily you may come upon the pads of the yellow pond lily. These are much larger and have sort of a heart-shape to them. They tend to grow in more shallow water and are hard to get to in anything but a canoe.

The flowers of the yellow pond lily are about the size of a golf ball and are usually held above the water on long stems. A shallow area of a lake with a thick growth of yellow pond lilies in it has a decidedly tropical look to it, so you are in for a real treat if you should find such a place. While the blossoms do have a scent, it is nothing like that of the fragrant water lily.

The final water lily, called the "water shield," is probably the most abundant as far as lily pads goes, but the flower is hardly a head turner. In fact the flower is so unremarkable that it does not appear in any of the flower books. Fortunately, my brother Tom is a wetlands specialist and he very quickly gave me the correct common name of this plant.

The elliptical leaves of this plant are about the size of a goose egg and float at the end of very long stems. Of all of the water lilies, this is the one that can live in the deepest water. The flower is a small, brownish cone that is held just above the surface of the water. Anyone who remembers the essay I did on the skunk cabbage will say, "Ah yes, that's right!" when they hear that this cone is referred to as a *spadix*.

Finally, as you patrol the shallow waters of a pond, you should have no trouble seeing groups of eastern painted turtles sunning themselves on rocks and floating logs. They are often quite shy and will dive into the water when you are still far away. Eventually, if you are willing to sit quietly and wait patiently, you will be able to get close to one.

Summer is also a great time of year for seeing baby birds, particularly in the bushes and weeds at the edge of the water. Adult birds may be a little more alert than normal, but your presence will not prevent them from tending to their little ones.

Floating in a canoe is much like driving in a car in the sense that many animals do not seem to immediately recognize us as humans. If you can move your canoe with a minimum of arm waving and splashing, most animals will not be too concerned until you are right on top of them.

Almost everyone I have talked to has at least one story of a great canoe ride. Sometimes the story is of an outing that took place years ago, but that is the beauty of the canoe—there is a certain quality to the experience that finds a permanent place in your heart and imagination.

Ferns

I WAS OUT FOR A WALK in the woods one day and when I bent down to re-tie my shoelaces I found myself staring at a fern. It was just a simple little woodfern, but it got me to thinking. I looked around at the luxurious carpet of ferns growing beneath the trees and I started to consider their amazing role in the Plant Kingdom's colonization of land.

The first plants to evolve on Earth were the algae. They appeared about 700 million years ago and they were totally dependant on an aquatic environment for their survival. This left a great expanse of habitat (dry land) open for the next new form of plants: the mosses.

Eventually, mosses were able to spread out across some of the landscape, but some serious challenges persisted. Unequipped with roots, the mosses were still dependent upon large amounts of water for their growth and reproduction. They were able to spread across the land, but they had to remain small and grew low to the ground so they would not dry out.

This still left a huge amount of habitat unoccupied, but Nature had plenty of time to find an answer to the problem. Finally, after more than 300 million years of experimentation, the process of evolution found the solution - the vascular plants. They would change the face of Earth forever.

Marvels of engineering, these new plants could actively transport water through systems of pipes and tubes similar to the arteries and veins of animals. Finally, plants could spread out across the land, and the first of the vascular plants were the ferns. As it turned out, they were a great success.

At this point in history, about 350 million years ago, there was still only one great super-continent known as *Pangea*. The tropical region of this continent was warm, water was plentiful, there was little seasonal variation in temperature, and much of the land was low and covered with great swamps. Basically, the world was a big, humid greenhouse . . . paradise for ferns.

Some species grew to the size of trees, and even today there are tropical ferns that grow to a height of 80 feet or more. The ferns grew in such abundance that their remains later became vast deposits of carbon-rich coal. Their impact was so great that that we even refer to this time period as the *Carboniferous Period*. Ferns reigned as the supreme form of plant life 165 million years before the first flowering plants appeared, and even though the flowering plants have since usurped control as the dominant form of plant life, ferns are still with us.

A fern is a plant familiar to most of us. Each plant has roots, a stem (known as a *stipe*), and leaves (known as *pinnae*). The portion of the plant covered with leaves is known as a *frond*. They look like modern plants, but hold on to their ancient habits in ways that are quite astounding. Fern reproduction, for instance, is sexual rather than asexual, but it is almost more complex than that of the higher animal forms.

The plants we recognize as "adult" ferns are neither male nor female. All are capable of reproduction, but none need other ferns to pull it off. These ferns are all *diploid,* which means that they have a full compliment of chromosomes in all of their cells. Flowering plants and all of the higher animals are also diploid.

To create a new life through sexual reproduction, most diploid life forms produce special cells with only half of the necessary chromosomes. These cells are known as *haploid* cells. It is easy to remember if you think of them as being "half ploid," but take out the letters "l" and "f." Female organisms produce eggs, males produce sperm, and when the two kinds of cells are combined they produce a new organism with a complete, but unique combination of chromosomes.

Fern reproduction has and extra step, however. Each adult fern produces millions and millions of haploid cells, called *spores.* There are many different ways that ferns store and disperse these spores, and this can be a great key in distinguishing between the different species.

Some, like the cinnamon fern or the royal fern, produce separate stalks with clusters of spore cases at the ends. Cinnamon ferns produce rusty orange spore cases, while those of the royal fern are green. Other ferns produce their spores in small structures called *frutoids,* which grow along the undersides of the leaves. These structures hold the spores until dry weather prevails, and then the frutiods, or other spore producing bodies, split open and release the spores into the air.

The spores are self-sufficient and do not need to combine with other spores to survive. If a spore lands in a favorable spot it will grow into one of two different forms. Half of these new plants grow single, heart-shaped leaves that will eventually produce both sperm and egg cells. The other half produce single, strap-shaped leaves that are that will produce only sperm cells.

These two forms grow to a maximum size of a quarter of an inch and are rarely noticed. They are completely independent of one another, but they usually grow close together. On rainy days when there is plenty of water, the sperm cells are released to find eggs. When egg and sperm cells from the same species finally encounter one another, they join in the process of fertilization and eventually give rise to the more familiar plant that we would all recognize as a fern. Wow!

There are about ten thousand species of ferns in the world, but eastern North America is home to only about one hundred species. All of them have the distinct forms that we recognize as ferns, but each also has the two other forms that are almost impossible to tell apart. So there are actually 300 different plants that make up the 100 different species.

So, I would definitely suggest that you take a closer look at the next ferns you see. They are an ancient life form, but they will never go out of style. To make things a little more interesting you should pick up a copy of *Peterson's Field Guide to Ferns,* which will give you a more detailed description of their life cycles and a very easy method for identifying the different species.

Then you can sit on the forest floor and thumb through your book while you gaze at one of these beautiful plants. If you sit quietly and open your mind to you may even find that you feel somewhat humble. After all, you will be sitting next to a fern - a form of life that had it all figured out more than 350 million years before you learned how to tie your shoes.

The Common Clearwing

O NE DAY, while exploring a field, I decided to sit down near a patch of spreading dogbane plants and just watch the world for a while. The flowers of the spreading dogbane are small, sweet, and they last for quite a while. They are also very popular with butterflies!

The patch that I was sitting near was a busy one. There were tiger swallowtails, red-spotted purples, white admirals, great spangled fritillaries, and even the occasional monarch butterfly here and there. There were also ctenuchid moths, bees, flies, and a whole bunch of insects I couldn't identify.

It was quite a show until I noticed another creature hovering around the flowers. I had been paying so much attention to the butterflies that I had probably overlooked this other visitor for some time, but once it had my attention it was all I could look at. Thank goodness I had my camera with me.

The animal I was looking at was another insect, a moth to be specific, but it was a species that stands by itself as being particularly un-moth-like. It was a common clearwing (*Hemaris thysbe*), better known as a hummingbird moth. Before I describe the moth, however, let's take a moment to look at the bird for which it was named.

There are about 320 species of hummingbirds in the world. Most of them live in tropical America and most of them are very small. The smallest hummingbird, the bee hummingbird of Cuba, is the smallest bird on Earth.

There are 20 species of hummingbirds that can be found in the United States, but in the east we have only one species, the ruby-throated hummingbird (*Archilochus colubris*). The ruby-throat is one of the smallest of the North American Species, with a body length of 3.5 inches and a wingspan of only 4.5 inches.

The one thing that sets hummingbirds apart from other birds is their lifestyle. They feed on nectar and small insects, and to do this they have become one of the most specialized groups of birds which exists.

In order to gain access to flowers hummingbirds have developed the ability to hover. While hovering, they can even fly backwards, a unique ability among birds. Hovering is no easy trick though. Bees, flies, and other insects can do it, but for a bird, even a small one, it requires a lot of energy. While hovering, the birds' wings beat about 55 times per second. While flying forward, this can increase to at least 75 beats per second. When wings move this fast they produces a droning, buzzing sound that we have called "humming." So now you know why hummingbirds hum. It's not because they don't know the words.

Because they are so tiny, hummingbirds often go unnoticed in gardens. They actually resemble big insects in a way, so it is even more curious that there is a big insect that resembles hummingbirds. The clearwing moth is about half the size of a ruby-throated hummingbird. It feeds on flower nectar, just like a hummingbird, and to do this is flies just like a hummingbird. Its wings are basically shaped the same as those of a hummingbird and they beat very quickly. This produces a humming sound very similar to that of a hummingbird, but much quieter.

Unlike a hummingbird, however, the wings of the moth are solid. They are covered with reddish-brown scales when the moth first emerges from its cocoon, but large numbers of them are shed during the first flight. The resulting clear patches make the moths' wings harder to see, and resulted in the name "clearwing."

So what is going on here? Is it possible that the moth is afforded some advantage by resembling a hummingbird, or is there nothing more going on than two different kinds of animals living a very similar life. To answer this you will have to consider the process of evolution.

Most people probably think of evolution as a process that makes animals different from one another. In the Galapagos Islands of Ecuador, for instance, there live some very famous finches which have adapted to just about every habitat available.

They probably originated from a common ancestor, and then broke off to form separate species in order to find enough room to live. Scientists refer to this as *divergent evolution,* a process where similar animals diverge from a common form to become new species.

But evolution can work in the other direction as well. Sometimes animals that start out very different can end up resembling one another because they have something in common. Take blue sharks and bottlenose dolphins as an example. Both are large, fast animals that live in the ocean. As a result they look very similar even though one is a fish and the other is a mammal. This is called *convergent evolution.*

Well, the same may be true with hummingbirds and clearwing moths. Both are small and both feed from flowers by hovering in front of them and sipping nectar. So it should come as no surprise that they look somewhat similar.

But I suspect that there is a little more going on here than that. I have a feeling that there is more than simple coincidence at work here. I think that the clearwing is realizing a benefit from looking like a hummingbird, and the evidence is rather interesting.

While the clearwing I saw was a reddish-brown, I have seen pictures of other clearwing species that are green in color. Could this be an attempt to look like a hummingbird? The clear panels on the wings also suggest that, although the moth cannot beat its wings 55 times per second, it would certainly like to appear as though it can. Again, like a hummingbird?

These things alone might not convince you, but there is one more item that I find particularly intriguing. If you look at the end of the clearwing's abdomen you will notice tufts of hairs which look something like tailfeathers. Well, moths don't have feathers, but the clearwing is definitely trying to look as though it does.

It certainly does seem that there is more than "simple" convergent evolution at work here. It may have started out that way, but at some point some of the moths were given an advantage for looking like hummingbirds. Once the moths started to make an "effort" to hummingbirds, the process shifted from convergent evolution to mimicry.

Now, I have had some training in genetics and evolution, but all of my training has merely given me the ability to make highly educated guesses. Do hummingbirds and clearwing moths look similar by accident, or is one animal trying to look like another? This is a very good question, but unfortunately I don't know the answer.

Keep a look out for clearwing moths in gardens of cultivated flowers. They fly between the moths of May and September. They are not always easy to find, but once you see one you are in for a real treat.

The American Beaver

HAVE YOU EVER NOTICED how many children love beavers? Charismatic animals, beavers live fascinating lives that seem to engage and entertain little kids. The wonder of beavers is not lost on adults, however. How many of you have ever spent a wonderful evening settling into a canoe and following a beaver around a quiet lake? Quite a few, if you are lucky.

There are some, however, who might view beavers as "problems." The thing that I'd like you all to try to remember is that beavers are not the sole source of these "problems." The driving force behind these problems is people.

Beavers are Nature's engineers. They are among a very select group of animals that are able to shape the landscape to suit their own needs. They build impressive dams that convert forested streams into ponds, providing habitat for themselves and countless other plants and animals.

Beaver ponds are not permanent, however. Eventually, when food becomes scarce, beavers will abandon their older ponds and build new ones in different locations. The old ponds eventually drain off when the abandoned dams fail, and they gradually grow into fields, meadows, and thickets as they are reforested. Each of these successional stages provides essential habitat for an amazing variety of plants and animals, including humans.

But why do beavers build dams in the first place? I think I may have the answer to this question, but it is a little tricky. It's sort of a "Which came first, the chicken or the egg?" kind of thing, so I'll try to explain carefully.

Beavers are rodents, and like most rodents they are vegetarians. In addition to cattails and other aquatic vegetation, beavers are also quite fond of the leaves and the inner bark (known as *cambium*) of many different trees. Beavers are not the only animals that do this, however. Porcupines, which are also rodents, are also quite fond of the leaves and cambium of many trees.

Porcupines are good climbers and they also have an impressive defensive mechanism (their quills) that helps to keep them safe from predators. Faced with the fact that porcupines were better suited for foraging up in trees, beavers had to come up with another strategy.

So beavers decided (in the evolutionary sense) that if they couldn't go up to their favorite food they would bring it down to them. Smaller trees from 2 to 6 inches in diameter are usually selected, but occasionally trees as large as 33 inches are cut. A beaver can fell a 5-inch willow tree in just 3 minutes.

This constant gnawing on wood causes severe tooth wear, and would eventually result in tooth loss and starvation in most other mammals, but beavers, like all rodents, have developed some very elegant adaptations to counteract these problems.

First of all, rodents have large incisors that grow continuously, preventing them from wearing down to nothing. Second, and more ingenious, rodents have evolved clever a mechanism for self-sharpening their incisors.

The teeth of most mammals, including humans, are comprised of two different materials: *dentine* and *enamel.* Enamel, which gives teeth their strength and hardness, covers human teeth rather uniformly and protects the softer dentine core. Rodent incisors are very different.

Instead of even layers of enamel and dentine, rodent incisors have a front layer of the harder enamel and a rear layer of the softer dentine. When rodents chew on things the two materials wear at different rates. The softer dentine wears faster than the enamel and the result is a set of razor-sharp, self-sharpening teeth.

Armed with these perfect cutting instruments, beavers cut down trees in order to reach the leaves and twigs that they like to eat. It is important to remember, however, that beavers are fairly large animals. The second largest rodents in existence, adult beavers normally weight between 45 and 60 pounds. Some rare giants have weighed in a 100 pounds or more!

Needless to say, large beavers living on a vegetarian diet will need a lot of food to survive. While there may be many foods for them to chose from during the summer months, their choices drop to just one during the winter — fresh twigs with green bark. There is a distinct problem with this, however. Wouldn't you agree?

It would be remarkably difficult for a beaver to cut down a frozen tree in the winter. Even if the beaver were successful, the dormant twigs would not provide enough food to make it worth the effort. So beavers had to come up with another idea. Their solution brings us back, full circle, to their dams.

In the process of cutting down trees and stripping the bark off branches beavers tend to end up with a huge supply of fresh sticks. Perfect as building material, beavers incorporate these sticks into their dams and lodges. Beavers then spend the fall months cutting additional trees and collecting the tender branches that they need for the winter.

To keep the branches fresh beavers take them down to the bottom of their ponds and shove the sticks into the mud near the entrances to their lodges. Slowly, the piles of food start growing, and since the pond water gets colder and colder as winter approaches the sticks are kept fresh. The stockpiling of food continues until ice completely covers the pond, and then the beavers can swim out under the ice and get something to eat whenever they are hungry.

Lodges are also essential for beaver survival. The entrances to the lodges are always underwater and must always be deep enough so that they will not be reached by the deepest ice of winter. This provides beavers with a safe home, which is well insulated from the cold and secure from predators, and access to fresh food as well.

Beavers have to be very careful when building their lodges, however. Any beaver that builds a pond that is too shallow will face starvation because their food is locked up in ice. Any beaver that builds a lodge with an entrance that is not deep enough will face starvation because the passages themselves become frozen, locking the beaver inside. Beavers must even build air vents into their lodges so they will not suffocate.

So, can you see where a problem lies? The problem is that humans, the most notorious habitat changers of them all, like to build things near streams and ponds too. It also seems that humans do not like to share.

Beavers are bound to the water by millions of years of evolution. To put it quite simply, they have nowhere else to turn for their lives. Damning streams and making ponds is what they do, so we have to give them a little slack. We humans, on the other hand, like to think of ourselves as intelligent and adaptive. We have learned to how to adapt to beavers by protecting roads with water-level regulators and our favorite trees with wire fencing, but we need to learn to adapt our thinking as well.

Beavers are not bad. They arc amazing animals with lives that have many parallels with our own. Perhaps, when we start to think that beavers are causing trouble, we should look at our own activities to determine who is actually to blame.

The American Toad

DO YOU HAVE A MOMENT? Good, let's go take a walk. I want to show you something. We're going down to that pond on the edge of town...you know the one. There's something really interesting happening at this time of year and I don't want you to miss it. What is it? Well, I was going to save it as a surprise, but I guess I can tell you now. The toads are breeding, and their songs are absolutely wonderful.

I imagine that everyone has seen a toad at one time or another. Toads like to live in cool, wet places like garages, gardens, and under the steps of the back porch. They do hop around a little bit during the day, but most of the activity in their lives occurs during the evening hours. The big exception to this, however, is their courtship.

As we get closer to the pond you will start to hear a wonderfully relaxing noise. It's a buzzy, two-toned trill that sounds like someone who is whistling and humming at the same time. It's a sound that has a mesmerizing quality to it, drawing you closer and closer and relaxing you at the same time. When you finally hear it you'll find that you could quite happily sit and listen to it for hours.

This enchanting music, heard day and night, is the courtship song of the male American toad (*Bufo americanus*). From April to July the normally terrestrial toads head for the water where the females will lay their eggs. Like frogs, toads are amphibians and their lives are tied to the water.

This may seem a bit surprising to you, probably because you have never seen toad in a pond, but don't feel bad. When you finally see the toads swimming around in the pond you will still think they are a little funny looking — and you will be correct. Whether they are on land, or in water, toads just look a little silly.

The silliness of their appearance is probably the result of the design of their bodies. Toads have very big eyes, very stout bodies, and an almost imperial manner with which they carry themselves. They sit upright, gaze at the world around them, and then when they finally move they propel their plump little bodies with deliberate little hops that can bring a smile to almost anyone's face. Toads have been described as "Good fairies in disguise," and small children are particularly susceptible to their charms.

But how much do you know about these gentle little creatures? Did you know that a toad might live to be 20-30 years old? Did you know that instead of drinking, toads sit in wet areas and soak up water through their skin? Perhaps I should start at the beginning of a toad's life so I don't miss anything important.

Every American toad starts its life in an egg. Unlike the eggs of frogs, which are laid in big clusters, toad eggs are connected in long chains like beads on a necklace. The chains of eggs are anchored to submerged plants and are clear at first. A few days after they are laid, however, the eggs will be covered with sediments and will be difficult to distinguish from the surrounding vegetation.

After only four days in the water the little toads are ready to emerge from their eggs, and then it becomes clear that a female

toad can lay thousands of eggs. The water will be swarming with little toads, but at this point they are little more than swimming em-
bryos. They don't even eat during these first few days because they
don't have mouths. Instead, they just float quietly and grow.

After six days (ten days after the eggs were laid) the little toads
have proper mouths armed with tiny jaws. At this point they have
become *pollywogs* and they immediately start grazing on the algae
and small animals that cling to the surfaces of plants and rocks.
Once they start eating, they grow quickly.

All this while, they breathe with their gills which are hidden
under a thin membrane on either side of their bodies. Water is
drawn in through their nostrils, over the gills, and is expelled
through a small opening on the left side of the body. This arrange-
ment allows the little toads to eat continuously without having to
stop to breathe.

Eventually, legs start to develop. Only the hind legs are visible, however, because the front legs are growing under the mem-
branes that cover the gills. At the same time the toads are developing lungs and as soon as their front legs burst through the skin
on the side of the body the little toads are ready to start their lives
on land.

Few things are quite as adorable as baby toads. The size of
your thumbnail, they have an innocence about them that is amus-
ingly at odds with their imperial little attitudes. Baby toads are in
a great deal of danger, however, for there are many animals that
appreciate their food value rather than their appearance. Snakes
(garter snakes in particular) are especially dangerous to small toads.

Toads have developed two methods of defense against predators. First, if they are picked up roughly, they will extrude a clear,
odorless liquid that is commonly mistaken for "pee." It is really
nothing more than water, but it works pretty well doesn't it? How
many of you have released a toad the instant you got "peed" on?

The second defense is poison, which is extruded from the warty structures on their skin. Toads release this poison when they are in pain, which is usually the result of being picked up in the mouth of a predator. The poison is particularly effective against mammals and has a convulsive effect on the heart and lungs. It has no effect on snakes, however.

If you are gentle, you can pick up a toad and admire it. No, you won't get warts! You may even find yourself having a little conversation with your captive. Grasp a toad with your index finger and thumb under its armpits, lift it up, and the toad will probably make a gentle trilling noise. Basically the toad is saying, "Hey, let me go!"

Anyone who has a garden should be thrilled to see a toad because they eat many of the invertebrates that damage cultivated plants. Toads are particularly fond of slugs and sowbugs, but they will basically eat anything that they can catch. They do most of their foraging at night, however, so don't be disappointed if your toads seem to be relaxing all day.

May and June provide the best window of time to head over to that pond on the edge of town (you know the one) and look for toads. They are not at all shy about singing right in front of you, and you will be able to identify the males in one of two ways. Singing males have huge throat pouches that blow up like balloons when they sing. These pouches can actually be larger than the males' heads, so they won't be hard to notice.

Males that aren't singing can be identified by their black throats (females have light-colored throats.) If you should find yourself next to a pool full of breeding toads, you may discover that you become very calm and relaxed after only a few minutes. I once sat by a pond for two hours, simply listening to the songs of the toads and thinking how great life was that day.

The Painted Turtle

I took a walk the other day, as I often do, and decided to stop by the shore of a local pond (another thing I often do.) I looked out across the water with my binoculars and it didn't take me long to notice that there were turtles everywhere!

They were all eastern painted turtles (*Chrysemys picta*) and they were all out sunning themselves. If you will allow me to anthropomorphize just a bit I would even say that they all looked quite comfy. Painted turtles love the sun.

For humans, this kind of activity is merely recreational. Sure, there may be some therapeutic value to getting away for an afternoon and just relaxing, but none of us actually need to soak up the heat of the sun for hour after hour.

In fact, there are generally no birds or mammals that need to bake in the sun. Birds and mammals are commonly known as being warm blooded. We can all generate our own body heat internally, so, in scientific terms we are known as being *endothermic*.

There are other terrestrial vertebrates, however, which cannot generate body heat. Snakes, frogs, salamanders, and turtles—the reptiles and amphibians—rely on external heat from the environment to warm their bodies. Thus, in scientific terms they are known as being *exothermic.*

So warm, sunny weather is more than just good for reptiles and amphibians—it is essential. Warm weather allows the temperatures of lakes and ponds rise, which, in turn, warm the bodies of the exothermic animals living in them. This makes it easier for these animals to remain active and helps the younger animals grow quickly.

But let me back up for just a moment. All of the turtle lovers out there are probably getting close to pulling their hair out because I am being a bit too general. So let me explain to the rest of you how I am torturing these poor people before they do any permanent damage to themselves.

The eastern painted turtle is a common, widespread species which has an enormous range that stretches from Maine, south to Georgia, and then west along the Canadian border all the way to the coasts of Washington and Oregon. This giant wedge-shaped range makes the painted turtle the most widely spread turtle in the United States.

Because they are small, slow moving reptiles, however, the painted turtles in the eastern part of the country never meet painted turtles from the south, the midlands, and the west (notice how I have so cleverly named the four subspecies without being too obvious?)

As a result of this, and as a result of the fact that eastern painted turtles live in a landscape which is quite different than that inhabited by the midland, southern, or western varieties, they also differ slightly in appearance. They are beginning to form separate species, but that may take another million years or so.

Everybody knows that turtles have shells, but does everybody know what the shells are? It has been my experience that people generally don't know, so here is what I am going to do. I am going to review the anatomy of a turtle and as I am doing this I am going to describe the field markings of the eastern painted turtle.

Turtle shells are actually the highly specialized bones of the ribcage and vertebral column. With this in mind you will realize that there is no way that you could scare a turtle out of its shell!! The top of the shell is a structure known as the *carapace*. If you look closely at the carapace of a turtle you will notice that it is broken into panels or sections. These sections are known as *scutes*.

You will also notice that the scutes are not just randomly placed or randomly shaped. There is a definite symmetry, just as there is symmetry in the human backbone and ribcage. There is a group of scutes running down the middle of the back which are known as *vertebral scutes*.

These are the specialized bones of the backbone. In some turtles they might have a raised ridge, or a *keel* on them, but they are flat and smooth in painted turtles.

Along each side of the vertebral scutes are another group known as *costal scutes*. These are specialized ribs which have flattened out and fused together to provide protection. The vertebral and costal scutes of eastern painted turtles are generally black and are edged with olive.

A line of small scutes runs along the outer edge of the carapace. These are known as *marginal scutes* and they are usually marked with bright red. These red markings, together with the red and yellow markings on the head and legs, are what prompted the name "painted" turtle.

There is only one other scute on the carapace that stands out from the rest. It is very small and is located in the center of the shell directly above the turtle's neck. It is actually smaller than the marginal scutes, and it is odd in the sense that there is only one. Called a *nuchal scute* it is probably an extension of the vertebral column. You would actually have to have a turtle in your hand to see it.

The bottom portion of a turtle's shell is known as the *plastron.* Because there is no backbone which needs to be accommodated there are just two rows of scutes that run the length of the body. Each scute is different from the one above or below it, and each has a symmetrical mirror image next to it. The scutes in the plastron of the eastern painted turtle are yellow.

Shells provide turtles with protection. A painted turtle can pull is head, legs, and tail into its shell so that there is very little for a predator to try to get hold of. This is the primary function of shells.

Shells also act as great solar panels too! Any turtle basking in the sun is likely to have the collected heat evenly distributed through its body because the scutes heat up evenly. This is a good thing for an animal which depends on energy from the sun to warm its body so it can be more active.

But the shells of turtles can also help us to differentiate between males and females. How does this work? Well, as with all animals that have different sexes the males and females have to get together, one way or another, in order to mate. For some animals this is fairly simple, but for turtles it is something of a challenge because their shells get in the way. But Nature always seems to find a way, right?

To facilitate the maneuver, the plastron on a male turtle's shell has become concave. As a result, it fits much better against the convex carapace of the female, and allows the male to get a better grip on her. In addition, male painted turtles also have very long claws which help them hold on to females more securely. But male painted turtles are not so driven by practicality that they overlook the more personal possibilities of romance.

Painted turtles have rather complex courtship rituals. A male turtle will even go so far as to face his sweetheart and caress her head and neck with his wonderful, long claws. Isn't that just the cutest thing you've ever heard?

Claws are easier to see from a distance, but you would definitely need a good pair of binoculars to see them clearly. If you can manage get hold of a turtle you should have no trouble determining its sex. Long claws and a concave plastron indicate a male. Short claws and a flat plastron indicate a female.

Catching a turtle is much easier said than done, however. If you have ever spent any time around a turtle pond then you will know that turtles have amazingly good vision. Turtles are also at their fastest when they have been out sunning them selves for a while. I actually had to spend several hours in a blind in order to get the photographs of turtles for the two turtle columns that appeared in *The Recorder.* Whenever I made the mistake of moving my camera too quickly I was rewarded with the spreading ripples of water which were the only clues that turtles ever been there just a moment earlier.

I have seen hundreds of turtles over the years, but one thing that I have never seen is a female painted turtle building a nest. It may actually surprise you to think of turtles in this way, but one of the characters which binds them to all other reptiles is the fact that female turtles have to lay eggs.

Turtle eggs are not hard, like those of a bird. Instead, they are softer, and have the texture of a very thick rubber glove. They also have to be kept relatively dry, so turtles cannot lay their eggs in water. So where does a female turtle leave her eggs where they will be safe from predators and also safe from the ravages of the sun? The answer is again a simple one: she puts them under ground.

Each year, from May to July, female painted turtles have to come out of the water and look for a good place to build a nest.

Thcy have to find areas of sandy soil which will be well-drained in order to keep the eggs from drowning, but areas that will also be moist enough to keep the eggs from drying out.

Once a spot has been chosen (don't ask me how it is done) a female will proceed to dig a nest hole, about four inches deep, with her hind legs. Into this hole she will lay up to 20 elliptical eggs which are each one and three-quarter inches long. The female then covers the nest with sand and has nothing more to do with her babies.

The eggs incubate for 10–11 weeks and hatch between August and October. The babies from earlier nests will dig their way to the surface and try to find water. Babies from late nests may simply spend the winter underground (somehow managing to survive the freezing temperatures of winter while only 4 inches from the surface of the ground) and emerge in the spring.

Each baby is equipped with a yolk sack which serves as a food supply for several days and allows the youngster to find water and food before running out of energy. When the little turtle finally does find water it will look for small animals to eat.

As the turtle grows to maturity (2-5 years for males, 4-8 for females) it will switch over from a carnivorous lifestyle to a vegetarian one. A full grown painted turtle can have a shell which is about 10 inches long.

Being vegetarians works well for painted turtles in the summer months, but it does present something of a problem for them in the winter. When the aquatic vegetation starts to die off in the fall, turtles find themselves with nothing to eat. In fact, they may have nothing to eat for 5 or 6 months.

How can a turtle live for 5 months without eating? Furthermore, where will a turtle spend the winter? These are all questions that painted turtles have answered in an amazing way!

Because they are cold-blooded (that's *exo*thermic) they use less energy when they are cold. They breathe slower, their hearts beat slower, and they sort of live slower. So, in the autumn, painted turtles take one last look at the world before burying themselves in the mud at the bottom of a pond.

They will stay there in a sort of suspended animation for the entire winter, not to reappear until the warm weather returns. During this time they have very few energy requirements, and are able to attain enough oxygen to live by absorbing it through their skin.

So, actually, it's no wonder that turtles enjoy basking in the sun so much. I imagine that if you had to spend the winter buried in cold mud you would take advantage of the warm weather yourself.

The Northern Pitcher Plant

ONE OF MY FAVORITE SAYINGS is that there is no better way to see something interesting than to sit down, lean against a tree, and wait for a while. Well, I wish that I could take credit for such an elegantly simple idea, but I cannot. Instead, I have to give the credit to my favorite nature writer, John Burroughs. The opening sentence of one of his most famous essays, "A Sharp Lookout," basically says it all: "One has only to sit down in the woods or the fields, or by the shore of the river or the lake, and nearly everything of interest will come round to him." Burroughs wrote this in 1882.

In a world that seems to move so quickly, where new technologies emerge weekly to replace last week's new technology, there is something comforting in the knowledge that Burroughs was correct. He had discovered one of the constants of the universe, and his words are still true more than 100 years later.

Now there are certainly times when I am looking for a particular bird or animal and I know just where to look. In fact, there are times when that is the only way to find what I am looking for. Oddly enough, however, it is usually during the quiet times when I sit and wait that I discover things. It was during one of these quiet moments that I found the subject of this chapter—the northern pitcher plant.

I had just started my summer working as an interpreter up in the Savoy Mountain State Forest and I drove by a spot called Tyler Swamp. For some reason I decided to turn around and take a look. So, I grabbed my binoculars, got out of the car, and stood by the side of the road for a while.

I heard a kingfisher, saw a butterfly, and then I saw something moving that looked interesting. With my binoculars I could see that it was a butterfly that I had seen before, but there, just behind the butterfly, was a pitcher plant.

I have only found pitcher plants a few times, but they always appear in the same type of habitat. Usually this is a swampy or a boggy area where there is a profusion of sphagnum moss. Where the sphagnum moss grows thickest there you can sometimes find a pitcher plant perched right on top of it. This was exactly how the Tyler Swamp pitcher plant was growing.

It is in these same kinds of conditions that nutrients are hard to come by. A thick mat of sphagnum moss growing in a very wet area may provide another plant with a nice wet place to put down roots, but there isn't going to be a lot of soil to root into.

Any plant growing in such a place will have plenty of sunlight for photosynthesis, but even though plants can make their own food, they still need some basic building blocks. Without them, survival is impossible. Plants usually attain these nutrients from the soil, so what is a pitcher plant to do? Well, there is always the possibility of improving the nutrient gathering abilities of roots to provide the base materials needed to sustain the plant. It just so happens that this is what pitcher plants can do.

But what happens during those times of the year when an abundance of food is required. Take, for example, the spring months when flowers need to be produced. What do you suppose a pitcher plant does when it needs extra food? Basically, it does the only thing it can...it kills and eats animals.

In the entire world there are only 450 species of plants that have evolved to be carnivorous. Perhaps the best known of these is the Venus' Flytrap with its active style of capturing prey. Pitcher plants, on the other hand, are what are known as "passive" predators.

Instead of having jaw-like leaves that grab prey, pitcher plants have turned their leaves into pitfall traps. It must have taken eons to evolve, but the design is wonderfully simple.

Each leaf grows in a tube-like fashion with one end open. On one side of tube there is a long, raised rib which acts as a support mechanism. In this manner, the open end of the tube-shaped leaf always points up.

At the top of each leaf there is an attractive hood which covers one half of the tube. The other side of the leaf has a pronounced lip which is covered with cells that secret a sweet nectar which acts as bait. The hood acts as a landing pad for insects that want to get at the nectar, but a closer look at this structure shows that it also has a much more practical purpose for the plant as well.

The entire surface of the hood is covered with hair-like structures that point down toward the open end of the tube. Any insects unfortunate enough to crawl down in to the tube will find it very difficult to climb out. To make things even more difficult for its prey, the pitcher plant has evolved a little surprise for its intended victims. In addition to the hairs on the hood, the inside of the tube is covered with cells that are sticky and easily shed by the plant. This results in an insect's climbing ability being further hampered because its feet are covered with what is effectively wax paper. Basically, any insect that goes down into a pitcher plant leaf is going to have a very difficult time getting out.

Since each of the leaves is always facing up, they also tend to fill with water. This is essential for the pitcher plant because it is important that the insects that become trapped inside the leaves drown before they use up all of their energy.

Once the insects die, bacteria that live in the small pools of water begin to break the insects down. In addition to the activities of the bacteria, the pitcher plants themselves secrete digestive enzymes that hasten the process. The cells which line the portion of the tube which contains water are then able to absorb the proteins, amino acids, vitamins, and minerals which are released by digestion.

The only portion of the insects that the plants cannot digest are the chitinous exoskeletons. As a result, pitcher plant leaves that are successful in capturing prey acquire quite a collection of exoskeletons at the very bottom of the tubes. Insects are not the only animals to fall victim to pitcher plants, however. Pitcher plants have also been known to kill spiders, mites, and even small frogs. This should be sufficiently gruesome to impress younger kids, so don't forget to mention it to any children you might know.

All of this activity is directed toward collecting enough energy to produce the impressive flowers of the pitcher plant, each of which has an appearance reminiscent of a sunflower. The large red flowers are located atop stems that can reach a height of 12 inches or more. The principal pollinators of the northern pitcher plant are large bumblebees.

If you know of some pitcher plants that grow close to your home you should definitely take an afternoon to go out and see the flowers. And, as with any time you go out into nature, do some exploring keep a sharp lookout.

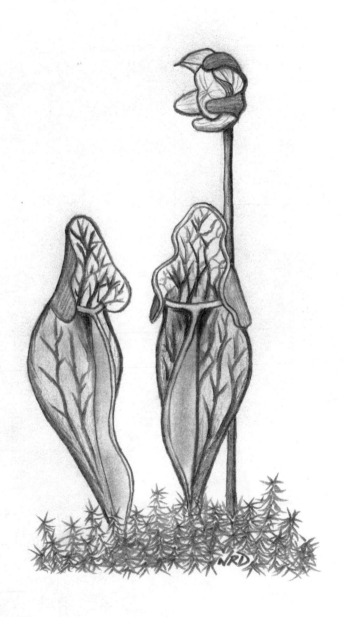

FALL

Life's Big Questions

I BECOME INTROSPECTIVE from time to time. Good or bad, it's a habit of mine that is quite beyond my control. I have no idea what plants the grains of life's big questions in my head, but like an oyster covering grit with layers of pearl, my mind tries to soften the edges of these questions with one thought after another, looking for the final, smooth, and lustrous answer.

The problem with life's big questions is that they have no right answers. The beauty of life's big questions is that they have no wrong answers either. They simply sit there, free of charge, and wait for you to contemplate their nature.

Autumn is the perfect season for such contemplation because it is a season of quiet sounds. Quiet sounds are the product of leisure and are thus few and far between. If you want to hear them you must find a special place, become part of the landscape, and wait. Do this and your mind will eventually drift to a question.

Everyone should take the time to sit and think now and then, so in the spirit of the season I am going to attempt to entice you into the forest by telling you a story. I am going to share the memories of a past autumn day with you in the hopes that you will set aside your weekend chores, even for just a little while, and go outside to relax. The story is my gift to you. The peace you find in it will be your gift to yourself.

It was a Saturday morning in October and I was up too early. I had volunteered to take part in a survey of white-tailed deer and gray squirrels, which sounded very exciting in the bright light of day, but I was learning that wildlife research often sounds more romantic than it actually is.

I didn't appreciate the fact that research which takes place at the crack of dawn requires that the researchers had to be up well before it. It was one of my first exercises in learning to endure pain, and in this case the pain in question was the pain of too little sleep. I cannot help but laugh about it now, but at the time I was misery incarnate.

It was 4:30 a.m. and I was dressed for a day in the cold — long johns under my pants, good boots, wool socks, several shirts of increasing thickness, gloves, vest, and hat. As I headed out the door of my U-Mass dorm room, quietly cursing my roommate who got to sleep late (Hello Rick!), I strapped on a small pack that contained a simple lunch of bread, cheese, and some beef jerky that my mother had made for me.

I set off on foot for the far end of campus where Holdsworth Hall was waiting for me. I was going to meet with a group of fellow crazies who had all forgone a comfortable Saturday morning to work with the U.S. Forest Service. Our mission was simple: go out to the Quabbin Reservoir's Prescott peninsula, walk slowly through the woods, and look for squirrels and deer.

To get to the Quabbin, we all piled into an ancient Jeep Cherokee, painted the hideous mint green of the Forest Service fleet, and headed out into the darkness of predawn. Some quiet conversation, a little half-hearted joking, and a great deal of yawning kept us awake as we made our journey.

Upon our arrival at the predetermined location, I was instructed to get out of the nice warm Cherokee, walk out into the woods, and wait for daylight. As I studied my map the Cherokee pulled away to deliver the rest of the crew to their respective spots. The taillights grew smaller, the sound of the engine faded, and I soon found that I was all alone.

Since I was the first to be dropped off, I had the longest wait. Time moves at a glacial pace when you are waiting for the sun, so I wandered into the forest by the light of a small flashlight, found the place where I was supposed to be, and curled up under a pine tree.

It was too cold to sleep, so I just waited. Fortunately, I was too tired to do anything but suffer in a semiconscious torpor. Contemplation of life's big questions at that point might have caused my brain to explode, rendering me useless for much of anything. Don't tell my parents, but this is the same condition I was usually in when I arrived at my Monday morning Chemistry lectures.

Anyway, dawn eventually arrived and shed enough light on the world so that I could start my work, brain still pretty much intact. My job was to walk quietly and deliberately down a predetermined path and observe. I was looking for those slight movements that are only seen out of the corner of your eye, and I was listening for quiet sounds.

My one-mile walk took me through the beautiful oak forests of the Quabbin. I passed old stone walls, red pine plantations, and the occasional beaver pond. I walked three steps, stopped, looked, listened, and continued on. While I was searching for animals with my eyes I was also listening for the quiet sounds of hooves on soft ground, or small claws on cold bark.

I took part in many such Saturday morning adventures, so I can't really tell you what I saw on this particular Saturday, but the thing that I do remember clearly is the end of that morning. It will be burned into my mind for as long as I live.

Being the first to be dropped off I was naturally the last to be picked up. This meant that I had a little while to wait before the old Cherokee came looking for me, so I found myself a comfy sugar maple and relaxed.

The day had gotten warmer so I had shed a flannel shirt or two, making them available as cushions for my head. Lying on the ground, again semi-conscious, but much happier about it, my mind was at peace. I heard the quiet sounds of leaves falling to the ground and the delicate sounds of a white-breasted nuthatch talking to itself as its claws found footholds in the bark of a cherry tree.

Then, as my mind drifted through the trees, I heard a noise so strange that my senses all came to full alert. Eyes open, staring at the sky, I saw a raven fly directly over my head. The noise that had captured my attention was the sound of raven wings cutting through the bright blue sky. Then, as if it knew it had interrupted my tranquil moment, the bird broke the silence with the croaking, laughing calls of a raven that knows it has just played a trick on someone. I can still remember those magical sounds as if I had heard them yesterday.

So this is what I want you to do on the next clear autumn day when you have a little time to spare: assemble yourself a simple picnic lunch, put on some warm clothes, and go and find yourself

MALE RED-WINGED BLACKBIRD
Could this male Red-winged Blackbird be admiring
his own reflection?

EASTERN GARTER SNAKE

Completely harmless to humans, the Eastern Garter Snake should be welcomed in any backyard.

AMERICAN BEAVER
While taking a break from dam building this
American Beaver snacks on a cattail leaf.

CLEARWING MOTH
Though it may resemble a hummingbird, the
Clearwing is really a moth that visits garden flowers
during the daylight hours.

AMERICAN TOAD
A male American Toad sings his peaceful trilling
song while sitting at the edge of a flooded field.

COMMON BURDOCK
Before it turns into a hitchhiker, the flower of the
Common Burdock is a favorite of many butterflies.

MONARCH BUTTERFLY
This Monarch Butterfly is feeding on aster flowers to fuel up for its amazing migration to Mexico.

a tree. Roll up a shirt, lay your head down, and close your eyes for a while. Listen for the quiet sounds of chipmunks looking for acorns, or chickadees looking for spiders in dry leaves, and allow your thoughts to wander. Sooner or later you will find yourself contemplating a big question and I guarantee you that you will feel relaxed and refreshed for the rest of the day.

Nuthatch Evolution

IT SEEMS AS THOUGH THE WEATHER has gotten all turned around and upside down during the past few years, so I can think of no better symbol for a sign of the times than a bird that defies the rules every day. I am speaking of the white-breasted nuthatch, an acrobatic little bird that can be found almost everywhere in eastern North America, and one that readily comes to feeders.

Identifying this bird is going to be very easy for you on the basis of its behavior alone. These birds can run down a tree trunk head first, and it is not unusual to find them perched effortlessly on the bottom of a tree limb, completely oblivious to the fact that they are upside down. As its name suggests, this bird has a bright white breast. What its name doesn't mention is the fact that it has a broad black stripe that covers the top of the head and neck, and a beautiful blue-gray back with hints of lavender and violet mixed in. Its black eyes are set in a face of pure white.

Another helpful characteristic is the shape of its body. The white-breasted nuthatch reminds me of a dart. Its long, thin bill comes to a pinpoint and its body it long and sleek. These little guys look like the sports cars of the bird world. Even when they are standing still they look like they are going 80 mph and when they finally do move it is effortless and quick.

Nuthatches are a great example of a group of birds that have been shaped to fit into a particular *niche* (pronounced nitch, or nish) by the process of evolution. In ecological terms, a niche is defined as being "the set of functional relationships of an organism to the environment it occupies." All scientific disciplines seem to enjoy creating words that they, and only they, can understand. This is sort of a job security ploy and to ensure their control over the situation the members of each discipline will endeavor to define their lingo in terms undecipherable to most other people. Thus, we get the less than helpful definition of a niche.

So let me help you break the lingo barrier. The set of "functional relationships" that define any niche can definitely be listed in a much friendlier manner. Basically, for any animal you need to answer these questions: where does it live, what does it eat, how does it catch its food, and where does it look for food? Find an answer for each and you suddenly have your list of functional relationships.

There is one important rule however. No two animals can live in the same place, eat the same food, look for food in the same place, and capture it in the same way. Each niche is unique, and only one animal can use it at any given time. If two animals try to use the same niche, competition ensues, and eventually one species will be forced out. If the refugee cannot find a new niche to fill, it will become extinct.

So let's examine the nuthatch niche and how it shaped this beautiful little bird. First, where does it live? Nuthatches, as a group, live in forested habitats. This offers no clues as to what a nuthatch might look like, however, since wild turkeys, wood ducks, and sharp-shinned hawks also live in forests, but remain very different in appearance. We still need more information. So we get the second bit of information, what it eats. The answer to this one is: insects. Nuthatches are also particularly fond of spiders, which they hunt during the winter.

Now we are getting somewhere. To catch spiders we can assume that this bird has to be small and nimble. It will not need webbed feet like a wood duck or hooked talons like a sharp-shinned hawk. But do we know if it is going to spend a lot of time on the ground, thus having big legs like a wild turkey, or up in trees, with smaller legs? Any guesses before I continue? Where do you think you would look for spiders in the winter?

Well, if I was a small bird looking for spiders in the wintertime I don't think I would look on the ground. Digging down to the ground through the deeper snows of a normal winter would not work for a little bird. So the answer is that the nuthatch has to look for food on trees above the snow.

I have spent a lot of time outside during the winter months and I don't recall seeing any spiders on the trees. Why would this be? Spiders are predators, but there is nothing for them to prey on in the winter because all of the other insects are either dead or dormant. So the spiders that survive the winter spend it in a dormant stage. This would make them easy pickings if they were out in the open, so they have to hide. So where would you hide if you were a small spider? The answer: in all the nooks and crannies on trees.

This leaves many choices, and thus many ways that a source of food could be divided. Nuthatches look for their food under flakes of bark on trees, while other birds look in old curled leaves or tufts of needles. To extract these spiders from their hiding places the nuthatch needs a thin, sharp bill like a pair of tweezers and relatively big eyes so it can closely examine all the possible spots. So we can see the nuthatch start to take shape, but there is still one last twist to this story. One that really shows the diversity and elegance of nature.

Tree bark can flake off in many ways. Pieces can curl up from the bottom, roll off from the top, or slough off from the side. So this still left at least two ways to divide a source of food, and two amazing little birds fought it out to see who would get what. Nuthatches focus their efforts on the bits of bark that roll off from the top, while the members of the creeper family (represented here in the northeast by the brown creeper) look under the bits that curl up from the bottom. Each will take anything they find under the bits that slough off from the side, but their competition for the same resource has created two distinctly different forms. The nuthatches spend a great deal of their time heading down the sides of trees, head first, while creepers move from the bottoms of trees to the tops.

Even among nuthatches there has been competition for food, and two species have emerged in the northeast. The white-breasted nuthatch specializes on deciduous trees (oaks, ashes, maples, etc.), while the red-breasted nuthatch specializes on the conifers (pines, firs, hemlocks, etc.) So keep an eye out for these little stunt-birds. Both can be seen in our area, but the white-breasted nuthatches are more likely to come to your feeders.

Burdocks

IT WAS ONE OF THOSE BEAUTIFUL DAYS, late in the fall, when the sky is blue, the air is cool, and the sun is warm. It was relatively early in the morning, and I had decided to do a little exploring in the cornfield across the street. There really wasn't much to see in the field, since it was full of the stubs of corn stalks, but the perimeter of the field looked promising. So I walked slowly and kept my eyes peeled. Every now and then I saw something interesting, but about three-quarters of the way around the field I really hit the jackpot.

There, surrounded by alder bushes, was a tiny manmade pond, which I had never seen from the road. The pond wasn't particularly active when I found it, but I could imagine how much activity might be there in the spring. So, feeling a certain amount of accomplishment, I continued on my way.

When I finally got home I felt pretty good because I had set out to find something interesting and I had found it. It wasn't until I went to untie my boots that I discovered that something interesting had found me. As I sat in my chair, I noticed that I had a hitchhiker on my leg. Staring at what had found me, I said "Finally!"

I then proceeded to untie my boots and I headed off for the kitchen to make myself a cup of tea to celebrate my victory.

So what do you think it was that had found me? Actually there is more that I need to add to that question. What do you suppose could have grabbed onto me and made me happy at the same time. No, it wasn't the girl next door. Shame on you!

What if I told you that it was a plant? I imagine that all of a sudden you know just what I am talking about. The thing that had hitched a ride on my pants was a burdock seedpod. Anyone who explores fields in the autumn either has had, or eventually will have, an encounter with a burdock plant. The tricky thing about burdock plants is that you never seem to see them. You simply look down at your legs and notice that they are covered with burdock pods. It's almost like magic.

Magic has nothing to do with it, however. Instead, we see yet another example of evolution hard at work. Burdock plants are using a method of seed dispersal that has been refined over the millennia, and at this point it works perfectly. The seedpods of burdock plants are covered with spines, but instead of being defensive spines, with sharp outward-pointing tips, the sharp tips are hooked. In the fall, when the plant has died and dried out, the hooks become hardened and can really latch on to a passing animal.

Once this happens, it is just a matter of time until the animal in question figures out what has happened and removes the bur. In the process, the bur breaks open and the seeds inside fall to the ground and wait for spring. When spring finally arrives the seeds will germinate and start the first phase of their lives. Burdocks are biennials, which means that they only live for two years. The first year is sort of quiet for the young plants.

Their large leaves (which remind me of rhubarb leaves) grow in a dense rosette close to the ground. The plants, which do not flower in this first year, put out as many leaves as possible in as compact a form as possible and they make food like crazy.

All of this food is stored in a large taproot that can be up to twelve inches in length. When the cold weather of autumn comes, the leaves die off, but the taproot remains alive. In this manner, burdock plants are setting the stage for a second year of life that is quite different from the first.

The following spring, the burdock plant has an enormous amount of stored resources to draw upon for its growth. Instead of growing low to the ground, the plant grows to be quite tall. The common burdock (*Arctium minus*) can grow to be four feet tall, while the great burdock (*Arctium lappa*) can reach eight feet in height.

In the summer, drawing on the energy stored in the taproot, these giant plants put out a huge number of beautiful pink and purple flowers. The flowers of the common burdock are on very short stalks positioned close to the large, alternate leaves. In contrast, the flowers of the giant burdock bloom at the end of long stalks that give them a very graceful look.

Burdock flowers resemble thistle flowers, but are much smaller. The presence of the hooked spines will also tell you that you are looking at a burdock plant and not a thistle. The hooks, though green and still somewhat supple, can easily cling to clothing, but the flowers are still firmly attached to the plant and will not come off until the fall.

Upon the arrival of the plant's second autumn the plant dies, having invested all of its resources into reproduction. The hardened hooks are now able to grab onto fur, clothing, and even the ridges of your fingerprints. Then, perched atop the very tall stem of the dead plant, the pods simply wait. Eventually an animal will stumble into them and they will break away from the dead plant with their precious cargo of embryonic burdock plants, bound for destinations unknown.

So how well does this method of seed dispersal work? Actually, it works very well! Burdock plants are natives of Europe, but as you can imagine they are not great swimmers. Instead they must have made their way across the ocean as seeds, safely tucked away in seedpods that were clinging to a cows, sheep, or colonists. Perhaps they were even stuck to sweaters that had been packed away in luggage of some kind.

I have found burdock pods on clothing that has been hanging in a closet for months, and taken them outside where they can germinate. This clinging ability also makes burdock pods a fun item to throw at your friends and family. I personally have sent many an unsuspecting friend home with a burdock pod stuck to the back of a jacket or a wool hat.

If you should happen to be out walking and look down to find your legs covered with burdock pods, try not to get upset. Instead, marvel at how amazing the pods really are. Thank the burdock plant for being the inspiration for Velcro.

Then, if it makes you feel better, wait until a friend turns the other way and then start throwing burdock pods. If you are really good, you can stick 10–20 pods onto the back of a jacket or a sweater, and your friend won't notice until he or she sits back in a chair, or a car seat, and then can't get up again.

The Eastern Chipmunk

A BIG PART OF BEING a wildlife biologist is being outside all of the time. This means that you have to adjust to different weather conditions, biting insects, and poison ivy. The animals are outside so you have to go outside. I have to admit, however, that I don't really enjoy working in the rain.

Now don't get me wrong, I love rainy days. I love hiking and canoeing in the rain, but I like to be able to get out of the rain whenever I want to. Walking out into the woods, well away from any trails, and trying to write on wet paper just isn't much fun. I guess I am just a "Singing in the Rain" kind of guy.

Knowing this about myself has given me a greater respect for the wild animals that have to live their lives come rain or shine. As I write this I am looking out at a rainy morning, sheltered but still close to the action. The forest has a very soft quality to it. The water has brought out the vibrant greens of the leaves by darkening the trunks of the trees, and as I sit here, hiding out, I am once again amazed by it all.

To my left, off in the fog, there is a wood thrush calling softly. To my right an American robin is digging through the leaves in an attempt to find something to eat, and above me, masked by the low clouds, a flock of evening grosbeaks has just passed by. They are off to some unknown destination and I would never have known they were there if the mist had not required that they call to one another so as not to get lost.

Perhaps the most comical character I see this morning is a chipmunk exploring for food. She is very watchful as she moves through the litter of the forest floor. She looks around for a moment, then explores the edges of a log. Then she looks around again before examining a promising clump of leaves under a bush. On a morning when I am hiding from the elements she is already set about the business of everyday life. I am almost embarrassed to admit that she is a tougher man than I am.

You may be wondering how I know she is a "she." What secret woods-lore have I acquired that has sharpened my senses to the point that I can determine the sex of a chipmunk at ten paces? Well, once again I owe it all to Burroughs.

The only skill I needed was that of being a good observer. I watched her mannerisms, I watched her movements, and I looked for patterns in her routine. And, oh yes, did I forget to mention that she has babies? I did? Well I guess that takes some of the magic out of it huh?

Yes, she has a little family. I noticed that there was one entrance to her underground world that she used more than the others, and then I noticed that hers was not the only head poking out of it. As she came and went I saw that tiny heads were venturing further and further out to take a peek at the world, and finally they made their great move out into the open.

Chipmunks are small ground squirrels that can be found throughout North America and Canada. There are a total of sixteen species of chipmunks on the continent, but the eastern U.S. has only one species, the eastern chipmunk. These animals are probably best known for their cheek pouches that they stuff full of nuts and seeds in the fall. In fact their Latin name (*Tamias striatus*) refers to this. In Latin, *Tamias* means "storer," and the full translation of the name is something like "striped storer."

Chipmunks live in elaborate tunnel systems that they excavate for many uses. There are chambers for sleeping, and latrines for cleanliness, but the most important use of these tunnels is food storage. Unlike the red squirrel and the gray squirrel, chipmunks are not particularly active during the winter. Instead, chipmunks become single minded in their efforts to gather as much food as they can in the autumn because once temperatures drop and the snow falls they seal themselves underground and do not emerge again until spring.

Upon emerging from their long rest they immediately get to the business of raising families. Mating occurs in the early spring, and each pregnant female eventually gives birth to three to five young in early May. The babies are born pink, naked, blind, and deaf, and about all they can do is nurse. They grow quickly, however, and in just a couple of weeks they look like little versions of their mothers.

Although they are ground squirrels, the baby chipmunks soon become quite comfortable climbing trees. They are weaned quickly and their increasing agility assists them in finding their own food. Chipmunks focus most of their efforts on seeds and nuts, but they will also eat flower buds, insects, snails, slugs, and even small mice from time to time.

All of their agility is needed to help them avoid their greatest predator, the long-tailed weasel. Foxes, hawks, bobcats, and the occasional snake will also prey on chipmunks, but the weasel is their most dangerous predator because a weasel can go anywhere a chipmunk can go. The chipmunk's best defense against these enemies is camouflage and noise.

Chipmunks are masters of blending in. Their rusty-colored fur is marked with black and white stripes that run along their sides and these stripes do a wonderful job of helping the animals become part of the background. When a chipmunk stands still it can be very hard to see it. Then there is that sharp voice they have. When a chipmunk gives a sharp "CHIP" and then disappears, you are often so surprised that you cannot figure out where the noise even came from in the first place.

This is a tremendous tool for avoiding weasels, but there is one predator that the chipmunk appears to be almost helpless against...the domestic cat. Chipmunks are easy prey for cats, particularly in the early summer when baby chipmunks are just starting their lives outside the safety of their natal dens. If a cat finds the entrance to a female's burrow it may kill every baby in just a matter of hours.

A well-fed house cat can afford to be patient because it isn't depending on killing for its food. Chipmunks represent nothing more than entertainment to a cat. When I was young I had many cats and my yard was always full of dead, uneaten chipmunks. In fact, my yard was a rather quiet place, because none of the species of small birds and animals that are normally willing to come quite close to people could survive.

If you have a cat I strongly urge you to keep it inside. It is safer for the cat and safer for all of the smaller animals in your yard. Just one or two weeks of no cat in the yard can produce an amazing difference in animal life, and one day you may even discover that a chipmunk is looking at you from your wood pile.

The Broad-Winged Hawk

THE SUMMER OF 2000 proved to be a rainy one — very, very rainy. As a result, those few evenings that were free of rain remain quite memorable to me. In particular I recall an evening when the sky was mostly clear, the air was still and balmy, and it was simply a pleasure to be outside.

As dusk drew near I had the wonderful opportunity to spend some time watching a young broad-winged hawk as it soared, circled, and called out across the forest over, and over, and over. Approaching its full independence, the bird was probably a little hungry, a little cranky, and may have been hoping to beg a meal from one of its parents.

Eventually the young hawk disappeared to the east, first drifting out of sight and then out of earshot. I never saw another hawk that evening, but it did get me thinking about broad-winged hawks in general. For those of you who have never seen one, a broad-winged hawk is best described as a small cousin of the red-tailed hawk. Both birds are members of a group of raptors known as *Buteos* (pronounced byoo-tee-ohs), which are characterized by their large, thick-set bodies, broad wings, and rounded, fan-shaped tails. Whereas the red-tailed hawk's most notable field characteristic is its red-orange tail, the broad-wing's tail (also its most notable field characteristic) is marked with thick, alternating bands of black and white.

The broad-wing's scientific name *(Buteo platypterus)* is actually one of the most literal and helpful of any I have ever seen. The genus name, *Buteo,* is the Latin word for "Buzzard." The species name, *platypterus,* is derived from the Greek words *platus,* which means "broad," and *pteros,* which means "winged." The full translation is "broad-winged buzzard," which is actually fairly helpful as Latin names go.

The buteos are the soaring hawks, and can spend effortless hours circling in the sky while they keep an eye out for the small animals which they prey upon. Red-tailed hawks are the largest buteos in our area, with a wingspan of up to 5 feet, and are able to tackle large prey animals such as muskrats and woodchucks. They are not limited to these larger animals, however, and will basically eat anything they can kill.

Broad-winged hawks are much smaller birds, with a wingspan of only 3 feet, and must therefore specialize a bit. As an example, it has been discovered that broad-winged hawks are quite partial to toads, which they hunt during the spring breeding season. They will also eat frogs, snakes, mice, voles, rabbits, chipmunks, squirrels, and small birds. As odd as it may sound, broad-winged hawks will even eat earthworms, which they may find in fields after a heavy rain.

Because of their reliance on smaller prey animals, many of which hibernate during the winter, broad-winged hawks are migratory. They spend the winter months as far south as northern Argentina, but are largely concentrated in Central America and northern South America. During our winter months, broad-winged

hawks are perhaps the single most abundant hawk in the woodlands of Panama and Costa Rica.

They reappear in eastern North America in early April and
begin a courtship that remains largely unknown to us. We do know
that the male will bring food to the female and present it to her
with some head bobbing. She may even bob her head back before
accepting the food from him. The pair may also spend time soaring in unison above their territory, but whatever is involved in their
courtship it doesn't take long. Often, the female will lay her eggs
just one week after her arrival.

Before she can lay her eggs, however, the female needs a nest
and I had the wonderful opportunity to visit a broad-winged hawk
nest in the summer of 2000. Brought to my attention by Dwight
Longval, of Conway, Massachusetts, it was the epitome of what a
broad-wing nest should look like.

A large mass of heavy sticks, the nest was located in the crotch
of a large yellow birch (a classic broad-winged nesting tree here in
New England.) Broad-winged hawks prefer to place their nests
high off the ground, but just below the canopy layer of overstory
trees in convenient 3- or 4-branch intersections. As a result, broad-
winged hawks usually choose their nest tree based on its characteristics rather than on its species.

Broad-winged hawks are very quiet and gentle birds, and as a
result they often go unnoticed while they are building their nests,
incubating their eggs, and raising their chicks. Dwight makes his
living as a Forester, managing forested properties owned by pri-
vate citizens. He happened to notice the nest while driving his skid-
der out of a client's property in Buckland, Massachusetts, and what
followed was a wonderful example of how responsible Foresters
work.

As a businessman, Dwight immediately recognized the fi-
nancial value of the broad-wing's nest tree. As a Steward of the

land and its inhabitants, however, Dwight found more value in the living tree. He decided to leave the big birch standing, and left several other valuable trees standing nearby, so that the broad-wings could raise their family in peace and security.

The female was able to lay her eggs and incubate them for a month while the male provided her with food. She was able to brood her chicks for two weeks until she joined her mate in the quest for food for their babies, and the two adults were able to bring their youngsters to the fledgling phase, all with no ill effects from the timber harvesting around them. By the time I made my visit to the nest there were two healthy youngsters perched in the tree, waiting for their parents to bring them something to eat. Their nest was just 200 feet from the logging road that Dwight had carefully routed around them.

In late August and through the month of September, broad-winged hawks will start to gather in huge flocks. On favorable days they will migrate en masse in large circling formations known as *kettles.* The hawks will search for thermals, invisible columns of warm air, which can lift the birds to incredible heights.

Once the hawks are satisfied with their altitude, they fix their wings and soar south, looking for new thermals all the while. In this manner they can cover great distances with very little effort. The amazing thing is that there can be thousands of hawks in a kettle. On September 14, 1979, a total of 21,448 broad-winged hawks passed over Hawk Mountain in Pennsylvania.

Keep your eyes peeled for broad-winged hawks in the latter half of August. Also, keep your ears peeled for their clear, two-note whistles. But be advised! Blue jays are particularly good at mimicking the calls of broad-winged hawks. I myself have been fooled into chasing after broad-winged blue jays many times and I always feel particularly foolish when I realize that I have been duped. I always feel like the victim of a practical joke!

The Blue Jay

A S A WILDLIFE REHABILITATOR I have had the great pleasure of raising many blue jays and I am always amazed at the malice and hate that people have toward them, particularly since this appears to be an animal that they know nothing about. Blue jays are seen as loud, obnoxious, and barbaric murderers, but I find it quite interesting that about half of the blue jays that I have cared for were very young birds that were caught and savagely injured by someone's cat. Cats exact a far more destructive toll on our local wildlife, but cat owners will often defend their own furry murderers while they denigrate wild animals.

John James Audubon (1785–1851) created a famous painting of three blue jays eating eggs and wrote of the blue jay: "Everywhere it manifests the same mischievous disposition. It imitates the cry of the sparrow hawk so perfectly that the little birds in the neighborhood hurry into thick coverts, and avoid what they believe to be the attack of that marauder." The painting depicts nothing more than a common occurrence in the life of blue jays, but has served to foster only ill will toward them.

To me, Audubon's comments serve as an illustration of the ignorance of man. It is true that blue jays eat the eggs and nestlings of other birds, and they are also very talented mimics that can flush out prey and enemies alike, but they do these things as tools for survival. The only real marauder was Audubon himself. He killed thousands of birds, including the poor "little birds in the neighborhood," just so that he could paint pictures of them.

Like their larger cousins (crows and ravens) blue jays are very intelligent animals. They have a tremendous "vocabulary" and although we do not yet understand what all of their noises mean, I am positive that they can say a great deal to one another.

Blue jays are also very family oriented. Starting in the spring, males and females both take part in some boisterous and energetic courtship rituals. One of the most conspicuous and entertaining of these is a behavior known as "Bobbing." Performed singly or in groups, bobbing is an exaggerated lifting and lowering of the entire body while singing a special song. Both sexes take part in this activity, and it is not uncommon to see several birds in a flock all bobbing as the same time. Should you ever see such a display you will probably end up laughing hysterically!

Interestingly enough, this loud and conspicuous courtship behavior takes part early in the year (February to April) and is all choreographed by a single female. The large flocks of birds are comprised mostly of males, all of which are competing for the female. The males do whatever the female does in an attempt to impress her. If she flies they fly. If she lands in a tree, they land in a tree. If she preens, they preen. It is the ultimate "Yes Dear."

Later in the season, when the majority of males have dropped out of the competition, courtship takes and interesting turn. Instead of loud and zany, blue jays show that they have a great capacity for gentleness and tenderness. The male will bring the female little morsels of food, and the female will sing little songs of thanks to him.

While all of this is going on the male and female share the duties of building a nest in a coniferous tree (pine, spruce or hemlock). Once complete, the female lays 4-5 greenish or bluish eggs that are spotted with brown. The female does the bulk of incubation while the male guards the female and provides her will all of her food.

When the eggs finally hatch, after 16-18 days of incubation, the male already has a great deal of practice in finding food. As the babies get older the female will start to gather food as well, and in just three weeks the babies are ready to fly. They do not fly far from mom and dad, however.

The life of a blue jay is complex and, as for humans, it is easier to learn the tricks of life from your parents rather than going off alone to learn by trial and error. Young blue jays often spend the entire winter with their parents, and this is particularly important for blue jays that are born in the most northerly portions of the blue jay range.

Blue jays born in Canada would have a poor chance of surviving the winter there because the environmental conditions are simply too harsh. So blue jays from the northern portions of the range often migrate south in huge flocks in search of milder weather. Some adults will stay behind, but the majority of birds migrate.

I remember one September afternoon that I spent on Spruce Hill, in the Savoy Mountain State Forest, watching the hawk migration. I also happened to notice that there were quite a number of blue jays passing by as well. By the time I stopped counting them I had recorded 147 blue jays! All were very quiet, and all were headed south.

As I mentioned before I have helped to raise many blue jays, and it is not uncommon to have an entire nest full of little babies brought in. They start out pink and helpless, but they grow quickly. As their new feathers grow they take on the appearance of adults, but like puppies they are silly and playful.

There is always one that is bossier than the others, one that is more shy and retiring, and the others are usually "normal," energetic little birds. But even at this young age you can see the intelligence within them. They are constantly exploring their surroundings and squabbling with one another over new objects.

With regards to people they are very trusting at first, but soon become quite aloof and independent. As soon as they can fly they venture off on their own, but they will often fly down from the trees just to see how things are going at home. They always have the same strong child-parent relationship toward me as they would have with their real parents and it is merely my inability to fly away with them that causes that relationship to finally end. If I had wings I would have a very large family indeed.

Blue jays do use some strong-arm tactics at bird feeders, but they are also willing to spend time searching for and driving off predators such as owls, hawks, and cats. Any ill effects that smaller birds may suffer at the feeder are more than compensated for by having many pairs of sharp eyes on the lookout.

Rather than finding the worst in blue jays, why not focus on the best? We cannot allow ourselves to hate an animal simply because we do not understand it. We should learn to open our eyes and learn the truth of things rather than subscribe to long held beliefs that are based on nothing but old opinions. Blue jays bring far more beauty into the world than they are given credit for and we should open our hearts to these wonderful birds and appreciate them for what they are.

The Monarch Butterfly

IF YOU CLIMB TO THE TOP of a relatively high mountain in September and look to the north you will have a fairly good chance of seeing hawks and falcons heading south for the winter. I have made many such trips to a mountaintop in the Savoy Mountain State Forest and I have seen many wonderful sights along the way.

One day I saw 374 broad-winged hawks fly by in just one hour! On other days I have seen American kestrels, peregrine falcons, merlins, osprey, red-tailed hawks, Cooper's hawks, and even bald eagles. Columbus day marks the height of the sharp-shinned hawk migration, and anyone who climbs to the top of a mountain ought to be able to see one of these beautiful birds fly by.

But if you remain particularly vigilant you might see another one of fall's migrants — a monarch butterfly. These amazing insects are headed for Mexico and they use the same strategies as the hawks and eagles.

On cool autumn days the sun heats the landscape unevenly. The areas which warm quicker create pockets of warm, rising air which are commonly known as *thermals*. Hawks and monarchs alike search for these thermals, and then ride the rising air as high as possible.

In many cases, the thermals will carry both birds and butterflies to altitudes of a mile or more before the thermals reach their upper limits. Then, with wings fixed, birds and butterflies alike will gently glide to the south, searching for the next thermal. In this way, substantial ground can be covered with minimal effort.

Now I don't know about you, but I find the idea that a butterfly can fly from Massachusetts to Mexico to be particularly amazing. Even more amazing is the fact that none of the monarchs that fly to Mexico have ever been there before.

The clincher, though, is this little factoid: no monarch that flies to Mexico will ever see Massachusetts again. To illustrate the amazing life cycle of monarch butterflies, why don't we start at the beginning.

In August, all across New England, monarch butterfly eggs start hatching. Each of the eggs was laid on a separate milkweed plant, which would serve as the young monarch's food supply.

Once free of the eggs, each of the tiny caterpillars starts eating...and growing. In just a couple of days the caterpillars grow to be too large for their skins, so they start the molting process.

Muscles flex and strain until their skins burst open, revealing fresh new skins which are decorated with beautiful black, white, and yellow stripes. These new skins have plenty of room for growth, and each caterpillar resumes eating.

But as the caterpillars get larger, and their intake of food increases, they have to be careful. Milkweed plants, the monarchs' sole source of food, are named for their thick white sap. Latex gives the sap its white color and makes the sap very sticky. In addition, the sap is also loaded with toxins.

Both the latex and the toxins are designed to act as protective measures against hungry insects, and both can cause death. The toxins kill chemically, and the sticky latex can suffocate unfortunate or careless insects that are covered with sap when they bite into a vein. But monarch caterpillars know how to avoid these problems.

Somewhere in their tiny brains, instructions for the safe consumption of milkweed are stored. These instructions direct the growing caterpillars to head for the stem of a milkweed leaf and chew through the veins that deliver the sap to the leaves.

With the flow of the sap reduced, the caterpillars can then devour the leaves with little danger of being sprayed with pressurized sap. They are also able to eat the leaves without receiving fatal doses of the toxins.

The toxins are, however, still rich enough to make the caterpillars themselves toxic. Any bird that tries to eat a monarch caterpillar will regret it, so the caterpillars decorate themselves with bright colors to advertise their toxicity. There is, after all, no benefit to being poisonous if you have to die in order to get your message across.

After several molts, the caterpillars eventually grow big enough to start the next phase of their lives. Each one finds a safe place, spins a little silken anchor chord for itself, and then sheds its skin one last time. What emerges is a beautiful green chrysalis, in which the caterpillar will change into a butterfly. This transformation only takes two weeks, and eventually, the new butterflies emerged.

Still toxic, the monarchs advertise their bitter taste with brilliant orange wings. This message is so effective that another species of butterfly, the viceroy, has even evolved to look just like the monarch. Careful observation will let you see that the black borders on the viceroys' wings are actually broader than those on the monarchs'. Monarchs also have many more white spots, but the similarities are enough to offer viceroy butterflies some protection.

The new monarch butterflies do not find milkweed flowers to feed on, however. Instead they find goldenrod and aster flowers which are abundant in the autumn. They loaded up on the nectar that will give them abundant energy, and then they head south.

The destination of every monarch migration is central Mexico, where all of the individuals of eastern North America congregate in fir forests. In all there are just nine congregation colonies, each containing millions of butterflies.

The monarchs will spend the winter months in these colonies, never eating, but just waiting. Then, sometime in February, the survivors will head north to search for milkweed plants. Males and females will mate on the way, and by the time the females reach the first milkweed plants in Texas, their eggs will be ready.

Once a female lays all of her eggs she will die, living only a few months as a butterfly. Her eggs will hatch, the caterpillars will grow, molt, and make the transformation to the butterfly phase. Males and females will mate, and the females will head north again, following a band of blooming milkweed flowers that moves to the north with the spring.

The egg laden female monarchs that finally reach Massachusetts may actually represent the third or fourth generation of monarchs for the year, each carrying instructions for the southward migration that they will never make.

Finally, sometime in August, a new generation of monarchs will hatch and grow. Instead of heading north and searching for milkweed flowers the butterflies will feed on goldenrods and asters and somehow they will know to head south instead of north.

And next year, if you are on top of things, you may even be standing at the summit of a high mountain, watching the monarchs fly by and cheering them on.

Signs of Winter

AT SOME POINT during the year it becomes clear to all of us that winter is just around the corner. It's no great surprise really, since it happens every year, but we all seem to react to it in the same way every time. "Is it really here already?, It's too soon for winter! I don't want it to snow!" Well, save your breath. There's nothing we can do about it.

The really big question is, how do we know? Some people may automatically say that you need only look at a calendar, but that would be cheating. I want to know how each and every one of us, without looking at a calendar, can tell that winter is coming. It turns out that the answer is really quite simple.

Even though we may not realize it, we are all in tune with the world outside. We can all look at certain aspects of the landscape and accurately tell what time of year it is, but since we always have a calendar around we never really pay that much attention.

Two of the seasons — summer and winter — are easy. Summer is a green month, whereas winter is a white one. Just look out the window and you can tell what time of year it is. Early fall is an easy one too. You say the trees have all turned bright colors? It must be early autumn. But as soon as the leaves fall, then what do we look for? What is it that tells us that winter is coming rather than going? This is where we start doing some detective work.

Since spring and fall are so similar in appearance we will have to look for sings of the previous season to predict which one is on its way. This may sound a little silly, but hear me out. Let's say that it's Saturday and you are finishing off the last bowl of turkey soup made from Thanksgiving leftovers. Rather than just sitting around all day, you decide that taking a walk in the woods would be a nice idea. So you gather up the family and head for your favorite hiking trail. Now as soon as you get out onto the trail you will be bombarded with signs of the coming season.

Your first impression will probably be that there are no leaves on the trees. What you may quickly realize, however, is that there are a couple of trees that actually still do have leaves on them. Oak trees and American beech trees are famous for holding on to dead leaves throughout the winter.

Leaves of the various species of oak are all pretty similar at this time of year. They are a rich, dark chestnut brown and the leaf tissue itself is rather thick and stiff. The bark of oak trees is generally well textured and comes in shades of very dark grays and browns.

The leaves of beech trees, on the other hand, are much more delicate. They are paper-thin, and are very light in color, looking almost golden as they hang in the woods. The bark of the American beech is very smooth and light gray in color. Without even looking at the leaves closely you should be able to differentiate between oak and beech with these facts alone.

As winter approaches there will be many of these dead leaves hanging on the trees, but by the time spring is on the way, winter storms will have ripped the majority of leaves off the trees. So there you have it. Oak trees and beech trees with lots of dead leaves on them are a sure sign that winter is coming.

But even the leaves on the ground can help you determine what time of year it is. When the leaves first fall off the trees they form a thick, fluffy carpet on the forest floor. In addition, they still look just like they did when they were on the trees for the most part. As you are walking in the woods, take a look at the ground and carefully examine what you see.

Now consider what will happen to them when winter finally arrives. The fluffy, dry leaves will be covered with snow, and as anyone who has shoveled their driveway can tell you snow is heavy. Over the course of the winter, as the snow piles up, the leaves are going to be compressed.

By the time the last of winter's snow finally melts off in the spring, the leaves on the forest floor are going to have been pressed into a wet, flat sheet — almost like paper. If you are ever accidentally sucked into a time machine and dropped out into a forest with no leaves on the trees, but no snow on the ground, you now know that you can tell what time of year it is by looking at the leaves on the forest floor. If the leaves are fluffy then winter is coming. If the leaves are flat then winter has already gone.

What's another sign? Say that your favorite walking trail takes you by the edge of an old field. Instead of being dominated by trees, the edges of old fields are usually covered with a wide variety of shrubs and vines. Now how do you suppose these plants can tell you what time of year it is? Just look for berries.

The fruits of most shrubs in our area are very important food resources for many of the birds and mammals that stay here in the winter. As a result, there usually aren't too many left by the time spring rolls around, so the presence of berries and other fruits on shrubs is a good sign that winter is on the way.

Grapes, rose hips, poison ivy berries, pokeweed berries, and elderberries are all good signs that winter is on its way, but there are two species which stand out from all of the others. The berries of the bittersweet vine are bright red and easy to see this time of year. When the berries first appear they are covered with a three-parted, golden shell. By winter's end these shells are gone, along with most of the berries. The presence of the golden bittersweet husks is a tremendous sign that winter is coming.

Not to be confused with bittersweet are the fruits of the winterberry bush. These are a bright fire-engine red and are often used in holiday centerpieces. Look for winterberry bushes growing in wet, swampy areas which usually have some standing water. I found a forest of winterberry bushes at Hawley Bog in Hawley, Massachusetts, but you should be able to find some near your house if you look hard enough.

Remember too that there are many people who like to enjoy a good apple or pear when they go for a walk. Generally, the cores of these treats are tossed into the bushes, so keep a lookout for apple and pear trees that may have sprouted up. Shriveled apples or pears hanging in these trees are another good sign that winter is coming. There are many species of wildlife, including raccoons, coyotes, pine grosbeaks, wild turkeys, and deer, that will eat these treasures whenever they can find them. By the time the winter starts to thaw, there won't bee too many of these valuable fruits left.

Okay. You've gone on a walk and now you're back home, sitting in your favorite chair and enjoying a cup of hot chocolate (another sign that winter is coming.) As you look out the window to see what is going on at the birdfeeder, you notice, perhaps for the first time, that there has been a change.

Sitting under the feeder, or possibly hopping around and chasing one another, are some birds you haven't seen in a while. They are those little gray birds with the white bellies that look like Easter eggs that have been dipped in white paint. The dark-eyed juncos are back! And wait, what is that little brown bird with the black-and-white stripes and yellow spots on its head? It is a white-throated sparrow!

These are both species that occasionally breed in our area, but the majority of the breeding pairs head up into Canada. For the most part, these species are absent from all but the highest elevations in the summer time, and only appear in large numbers when the coming winter drives them south. As the millions of birds pass through our area, they are more than happy to stop at birdfeeders for a quick snack.

Some of the birds will stay with us through the winter, so their coming is a fairly good sign that winter is on the way. If you are lucky, you might have even seen a flock of snow buntings while you were out on your walk. Snow buntings only stray this far south when winter is approaching. They are lumped together with juncos in a group of birds known as "snow birds." If ever there was a sign of the coming winter, the arrival of snowbirds is surely it!

A much more obscure sign of the coming winter can be found in rural areas. You may have noticed that a new crop of saplings without any branches has been planted at intervals next to the roads. These were not placed where they can grow, but rather to serve as roadside markers for the plow drivers on dark winter nights. In area where there are few houses it can actually be quite difficult to figure out where the roads are after a big storm. Using saplings is a ecologically friendly way to keep the roadsides trimmed and keep the plow drivers safe at the same time.

The final, and perhaps most powerful, sign that winter is coming is the change in length of each day. The Earth is spinning as it orbits the sun and it completes one full revolution every twenty-four hours. We call each of these revolutions a "day." This would result in twelve hours of light, and twelve hours of darkness every day of the year, except for the fact that the axis of the Earth's spin is slightly tilted — twenty-three degrees to be exact.

So this means that at certain times of the year one or the other of the Earth's poles is pointing toward the sun more than the other. In the Northern Hemisphere, in the middle of June, the northern pole is pointed at the sun and we have the longest period of sunlight during the year.

After that, the period of sunlight decreases a little each day until the Earth has traveled half of its orbit. At that point the Earth is positioned so that the northern pole is pointing away from the sun. Then we have the shortest day of the year, less sunlight means less heat, and that is when winter is upon us.

So as you return from your walk you will probably notice that it is getting dark very early. The sun may set at 4:12 p.m., but if you live in the hills you may lose sight of it by as early as 3:30 p.m. Don't be too upset though, because soon you will be able to enjoy putting all of your new detective skills to use as you examine the signs of animal life in the snow.

The Red Squirrel

THE RED SQUIRREL *(Tamiasciurus hudsonicus)*, also known as the "chickaree" or "pine squirrel," is the second-smallest tree squirrel that can be found in the Northeast. Measuring in at a length of 11 to 15 inches, with a bushy tail accounting for 4 to 6 inches, the red squirrel is much smaller than its larger cousin the gray squirrel *(Sciurus carolinensis)*, and only slightly larger than the southern flying squirrel *(Glaucomys volans)*.

But the red squirrel makes up for its small stature with attitude. Weighing in at a diminutive 5-8 ounces, this little beast will reign supreme at any birdfeeder it decides to lay claim to. I have seen large gray squirrels, which can weigh up to 25 ounces or more, flee in terror of an enraged red squirrel. I just love red squirrels!

Even humans may be given a good scolding from time to time. This usually happens when a person, out for a nice walk through the woods, wanders past a red squirrel. It has happened to me many times and it always makes me laugh out loud.

One of these little guys will scamper down a tree to a safe branch about ten feet off the ground, and then proceed to unleash an amazing barrage of squeaks, whistles, and chatters while madly waving its little tail. If I could actually understand what the squirrel was saying I am quite sure I would blush.

But you have to admire the spirit of a tiny little animal that won't take any nonsense from anybody. The other nice thing about their scoldings is that they will come quite close where you can get a good look at them.

The first characteristic that most people notice about red squirrels is their eyes. It usually surprises people to notice that they have such pronounced white eye rings. I think they are quite lovely, and nicely set off their shiny black eyes. In fact, their eyes are so shiny, that I could actually see my reflection in the eye of a squirrel I once photographed.

The red squirrel got its name for its beautiful winter coat, which is truly spectacular when illuminated by direct sunlight. In the summer the rich orange-red fur on the back and tail will fade to more closely match the brown fur of the flanks, but it still retains a hint of orange.

It is important that the fur on the red squirrel's tail match the rest of its body because the tail is actually used as a defense mechanism. If you look at a squirrel you will notice that its tail is roughly the same size and shape as its body. This is no accident.

If you watch a squirrel as it sits in a tree and surveys its surroundings for predators, you will often notice that it will twitch its tail from time to time. Did you ever wonder why?

Well, most *diurnal* predators (predators that are active in the daytime) locate their prey by keying in on movement. So if a squirrel can carry around a squirrel-sized dummy of itself and wave it in the air, it is more likely that a predator sneaking up on the squirrel will strike at the tail instead of its body.

Predators usually get only one shot at a prey animal and if they do not grasp their intended victim firmly it will get away. Gray squirrels are particularly good at drawing attention to their tails, but red squirrels aren't too bad either.

It is important to remember, however, that red squirrels are very aggressive little beasts and they fight amongst themselves quite savagely at times. Sometimes parts of tails are bitten off in these fights, and that is why some individuals will have oddly short tails.

The fighting is most severe in the late winter when the males are competing for the attentions of the females. When two males are fighting there is often a lightning fast chase around a tree until one male tackles another. But males will also pursue female red squirrels in much less aggressive nuptial chases that can be quite elaborate.

I have watched these much more friendly games of tag last for twenty minutes or more, and I must admit that both the males and females look as though they are having a good time. The next time you see a chase try to decide if it's a fight between angry males, or a romantic game of tag.

After mating, the female heads off on her own to prepare a nest for her babies. The male has no further role in family life. The most attractive location for a nursery nest is inside a hollow tree. Here the female will build a warm nest, often using the shredded bark of grapevines.

Her babies will be born in late March or April after a gestation period of about 48 days. The typical litter contains 3 to 7 babies, and they are born naked, blind, and helpless. They grow a light layer of fur at about 10 days of age, but their eyes remain closed for a full month. Once their eyes open, the little squirrels immediately begin to explore, but they will not be weaned from their mother until they are two months old. They will stay with her until late summer, when she may have a second litter.

Young squirrels learn what is good to eat from their mothers, and once they have done their research they start preparing for winter. Whereas gray squirrels specialize on deciduous forests, red squirrels like to live in conifers. They harvest the cones from spruce and pine trees, each of which may contain up to 50 seeds.

Red squirrels will often store these cones in huge piles on the ground, which they will then visit throughout the winter. People who hike or ski in the woods during the winter may come upon huge piles of pine cone scales where the squirrels sit and eat. These big compost piles are referred to as middens.

Red squirrels will also readily come to bird feeders for sunflower seeds, but two of their most favorite foods are actually quite surprising. The first of these is mushrooms, which red squirrels will actually pick whole and hang in trees to dry. Even the deadly amanita mushrooms, which are quite poisonous to humans, are savored by red squirrels.

Their other favorite food is one that many people also enjoy—maple sap. I once lived in a house that had a big sugar maple next to a window. One Spring I noticed that the resident red squirrels had tapped into the tree for the sap by going out to some of the smaller branches and gnawing off the bark so the sap would flow freely. All of the squirrels, and even some of the chickadees in my yard visited this particular branch to take sips of the sweet treat.

The next time you are hiking through a forest of hemlocks and pines, be sure to listen for the scolding calls of the little red squirrel. If you should happen to be assaulted with a particularly severe barrage, take a careful look at the trees around you. If it is early in the summer, and if you are in the right place, you may notice that there are a bunch of baby squirrels looking on with great curiosity as their loving mother attempts to scare you away.

Poison Ivy

POISON IVY IS A PLANT that has taken on an almost mythic quality. Everyone knows what it will do to a careless hiker, gardener, or athlete, but no one really seems to know what it looks like. They know that its is out there somewhere, yet the proper and timely identification of the plant has never been learned.

Winter is not a time of year that is normally associated with poison ivy, but a careless person can run into trouble at any time of year when poison ivy is involved. What you may not know is that poison ivy is also a remarkably popular source of food for many of our local birds. So now you have two good reasons to learn what poison ivy looks like: self-preservation and birdwatching.

So, being the great guy I am, I have decided to be a real pal and give you an introductory course in poison ivy identification. Armed with the knowledge you are about to receive, you will have a much better chance of avoiding one of Nature's most unpleasant experiences...the horrible, burning and itching rash brought on by one of the greatest experiments with chemical warfare. For the purposes of incentive I will start with what poison ivy can do to you before I teach you how to identify it.

The active ingredient, to which we humans react so violently, is a chemical in the sap of the poison ivy plant known as *urushiol.* Urushiol is a kind of oil that flows throughout the entire plant, but merely brushing against a poison ivy plant will not result in a terrible rash. As long as the urushiol stays inside the plant there is no problem. You actually have to mash the plant to get the sap on you.

If you have been careless, and the sap does get on you, the urushiol oil will soak in to your skin and get down into the lower dermal layer. Once its presence is detected, the human body will respond with an energetic assault by white blood cells. The skin then becomes inflamed, blisters start to form, and the worst part — the itching — sets in.

These blisters cannot spread poison ivy. They are simply a torturous byproduct of our bodies' attempts to rid themselves of a toxin. There are many ways to treat the symptoms of poison ivy, but one of the best is also one of the most satisfying. Wash the affected area with the hottest water you can stand. You can even scrub the area with a brush if you want. It hurts sometimes, but it also feels good at the same time. As John Cougar Mellencamp would say — It Hurts So Good! When you can stand the heat no longer, douse with rubbing alcohol. Poison ivy always lasts longer than you would like, but this treatment seems to make it go away faster.

Now you can avoid all of this unpleasantness if you are observant. Poison ivy is found in a ridiculously wide variety of habitats and it can take on many forms. Fortunately, however, the plant is also predictable. So I am going to describe a couple of the plant's most common forms, and which habitats they are found in.

The first, and probably the most dangerous form of poison ivy, is the one that grows in the grass next to parking lots, tennis courts, or roads. Poison ivy is also particularly fond of the poor soils next to old bridges and sidewalks, so look for it there too.

In these open situations poison ivy is usually a short stemmed plant about 6 to 12 inches in height. At the top of the single stem are three shiny leaves that have an oily-red appearance. There may be many of these stems in an area, but each one will have the characteristic single cluster of three shiny leaves.

The second, and also very common, form of poison ivy is one that grows along old barbed wire fences. Instead of being a short little plant, poison ivy takes on the form of a climbing vine. Here the plant will have a very thick stem covered with dark-brown hairs. The stems become branches that can reach up to two feet in length, but they still have the three shiny leaves at the ends. Again, the leaves are shiny in appearance because they have grown out in the open.

The third form of poison ivy is much less common because it is found in forests. These are usually very old plants that have grown along with the trees, and have reached heights of up to forty feet. Just look for the dark-brown, hairy vines climbing up very large trees. In forests, out of the direct sunlight, poison ivy leaves are usually the same flat green of any other plant.

As far as I can tell, the fourth form of poison ivy is only found on the coast. In the open sandy habitats of the back dune areas, I have seen poison ivy grow as an erect shrub with no other plants providing support. These shrubs can grow to be twenty feet tall and, as a ranger for the National Park Service, I remember seeing little kids diving into such bushes while playing army games. I saw adults wading into these bushes in order to hang wet towels to dry. I could barely stand to watch this happen, but it was amazing how many of these people ignored my warnings.

To avoid getting into poison ivy you simply have to look for a plant that has slender gray stems and three leaves. The leaves can be shiny or dull, they can have smooth or toothed edges, and they can be at ground level or up in the trees. As long as you pay attention you should have no problem.

As luck would have it, we humans are the only animals that are allergic to urushiol oil. In fact, poison ivy berries (which must be packed with urushiol) are a favored food source for over sixty species of birds. Since the seeds in the berries pass through the digestive systems of birds unharmed, birds act as the chief planting agents for new poison ivy plants.

While we have to avoid poison ivy, it shouldn't be a problem for us if we stay alert. I would suggest that you go outside and see if you can find some poison ivy in any of the situations I have described. Once you have really noticed it, you will find that you begin to see it everywhere. Hopefully, you will be able to avoid it too!

The Common Raven

I WAS SITTING IN MY LIVING ROOM, reading a book by the fireplace, when I heard it — the call of a raven. I was quite surprised really, not because I was hearing a raven, but rather that I was able to hear the raven while I was inside. None of the other noises outside seemed able to penetrate the walls or window glass, but the raven's call came right on in.

I made a dash for the window, hoping to catch a glimpse of the bird, and there it was, soaring against the blue northern sky on a perfect cloudless day. The raven called again, began a gentle dive, and then called one last time before it disappeared behind a ridge top. It was a marvelous thing to see, but it has not always been an easy thing to see.

Long before the mighty Roman Empire had taken control of much of Europe, ravens had spread throughout the entire Northern Hemisphere. They lived in Asia, Africa, Europe, and North America, and in those days there probably weren't too many places where you couldn't find ravens. What a wonderful time that must have been.

Ravens make a living by following predatory animals and scavenging off the remains of their kills. Because of their huge range, ravens simply follow the predators that live where they happen to live. Wolves are just as good as lions, and bears are just as good as killer whales. As it happens, humans kill things too, and strange as it may seem there appears to be nothing humans enjoy more than killing each other. So, back in the days of the Romans, the Vikings, and King Richard II, large groups of humans would decide to kill each other whenever one group got mad at another.

Well, it made no difference to the ravens that humans were killing each other. To them dead soldiers were just food lying on the ground. Humans, however, didn't like to see ravens scavenging around their dead friends and they decided that ravens were evil. So, instead of putting an end to wars, which would have put an end to ravens scavenging off the dead, the Europeans decided to wage war on ravens. Ravens have been rare in Europe ever since.

This was not how every human culture saw things, however. Some native peoples of North America had a different kind of relationship with the Earth, and many of them saw the raven as the creator of the universe. As they saw it, ravens created the stars by flicking bits of mica into the sky, and they created humans out of dust for their own amusement.

It has even been suggested that ravens invented sex as a little joke that they played on humans. Ravens made it something that was enjoyable, but something they could also enjoy watching us bicker about. Ravens were revered and were not seen as evil — just mischievous.

Ravens had it pretty good here in North America until the Europeans arrived. As far as the colonists were concerned, the world was made for them to do with as they pleased. They hated ravens and bears and wolves, and attempted to kill them all. Let me just remind you that those "Europeans" were great grandfathers and great grandmothers for many of us...including me.

The end result was the complete removal of ravens from eastern North America and most of the west. It has only been during my lifetime that ravens have returned to New England. I never saw a raven when I was a kid. It wasn't until I was a teenager that I began to hear people whispering about ravens starting to reappear. Then, while I was working in the forests of the Quabbin Reservation, I finally saw my first raven.

I was in college, studying to be a wildlife biologist, and working as a forest technician for the U.S. Forest Service. I had been out doing wildlife surveys all morning and I had decided to sit down and lean against a tree while I waited for my ride. It was one of those perfect autumn days when the sky is a clear, dark blue, and it was very quiet. I was comfortably relaxed, sitting with my eyes closed and my back against a tree, when I heard this odd, rhythmic whistling sound. I opened my eyes, looked up, and there above me was a raven. The odd noise was the sound of the air rushing through its wings as it flew overhead. I will never forget that experience as long as I live.

Ravens were returning to the east along with another animal — the coyote. After all, ravens follow predators around, and coyotes were also making a comeback at the time. Today, coyotes are well established in the Northeast, and ravens are doing well too.

Worldwide, there are eight subspecies of the common raven *(Corvus corax)*. Basically, they are all the same bird with regional differences in size. In the North America there are only two subspecies, and here in the northeast the only raven you will see is *Corvus corax principalis,* one of the largest of the ravens. They are magnificent birds and I find it quite fitting that their scientific name, a mixture of Greek and Latin words, means "Imperial Raven."

Ravens and crows are very closely related. Both are large black birds, and on many occasions I have seen people point to a particularly large crow and proclaim it to be a raven. I suppose this is understandable, but once you actually see a raven you will notice one very important thing: ravens are huge!

With wing spans of up to four feet, and body weights in excess of 3.5 pounds (four times heavier that an American crow) ravens rank as the largest of all of the world's songbirds. Yet ravens don't sing, exactly. Instead, they talk. It has been suggested that ravens have a greater variety of calls than any other animal on Earth, with the sole exception of man.

Along with this extensive vocabulary and great intelligence ravens also appear to have a genuine interest in having fun. Ravens are well known for their habits of teasing large predatory animals, and one game that they are particularly fond of is "Tease the wolf." Both simple and daring, a raven that wants to play this game simply has to find a wolf which is eating a deer or a moose. Then the raven has to walk up behind the wolf and yank on its tail. Many wildlife researchers have witnessed this activity and all have come to the conclusion that the ravens are having a wonderful time.

Perhaps the most delightful account of ravens at play, however, was published in *National Geographic* magazine several years ago. A photographer had the unbelievable good fortune to witness a group of ravens sliding down a snow-covered hill. Each bird would take a turn by flipping over on its back and sliding down the little hill headfirst while the others stood and watched, croaking out their wonderful raven laughs. I am laughing at the very thought of it.

If you want to see a raven I would suggest that you spend a lot of time outside. Since ravens prefer to nest on rocky ledges, spending time on top of, or close to, a mountain with cliffs is a particularly good idea, but you can never tell where a raven will turn up. Just listen for a deep, wonderful croaking call and look for a big black bird with long primary feathers that look like fingers at the ends its wings. Ravens also have very large, heavy beaks and wedge-shaped tails — other important keys to their identification.

In contrast, crows have rounded, fan-shaped tails, smaller beaks, and are much smaller birds.

There were two raven photographs that I had considered for this book. The first was taken at the top of Mount Monadnock, in New Hampshire, and was the product of a physical and mental challenge more painful than any I have ever endured. In contrast, the second photo (which appears on the back cover) was taken at the top of Mount Holyoke, in Hadley, Massachusetts, and it was one of the easiest pictures I have ever taken. It seems that the ravens have been playing tricks on me too, but I love them just the same.

The American Crow

J AMES R. WALSH, of Greenfield, Massachusetts, once wrote to me and inquired about the difference between ravens and crows. It was a very good question, and proved to be the topic of two very successful newspaper columns, so I thought I should include both of them in this book. The previous chapter covered ravens. So, here is the follow up treatment for crows. James, this one's for you.

Crows and ravens are extremely complex and marvelous birds. Entire books have been dedicated to each of these birds, so it should come as no surprise that I cannot cover everything aspect of their lives in this short chapter. I will, however, attempt of cover those particulars that will give all of you an idea of what crows are like.

Worldwide, there are 45 species of birds which have been honored with the name "crow." There are a further 605 species which have been included in the *Corvidae* Family, but most of us would only recognize the 113 species of ravens, crows, and jays as true crows, so I'll stick with this smaller group.

Crows and ravens are very closely related and, with very few exceptions, they are large, intelligent, black birds. There are a very few species that have red or yellow beaks, a few which have white patches of feathers, and one that has red legs. In contrast, the jays of the world are all brightly colored blue and green birds, and very few of them have black or gray plumage. Like their larger cousins, however, jays are bouncy, energetic, sassy, and beautiful birds.

In northeastern United States there are only five *corvids* (as members of the *Corvidae* Family are known) which you are likely to see: the common raven, the American crow, the fish crow, the gray jay, and the blue jay. Fish crows are rarely seen too far from the ocean, but they will occasionally go on adventures and follow great rivers inland. Gray jays are rarely seen in any areas except the northernmost portions of Vermont, New Hampshire, and Maine. So if you are inland, and south of the Canadian border, there are only two crow-like birds you are likely to see — the common raven and the American crow.

The American crow is a large black bird with a body length ranging from 17 to 21 inches and a wingspan of 33 to 40 inches. In addition to being smaller than ravens their voices are higher in pitch, they have fan-shaped tails when seen in flight, and their primary feathers are much shorter. This last characteristic gives their wings a more even appearance in flight, unlike the long "fingered" wings of ravens.

Like ravens, however, the glossy black feathers of crows have a gorgeous blue-green-violet iridescence when see up close and in the proper light. Any people who get close enough see these colors in a crow's feathers should consider themselves fortunate indeed.

Probably one of the best known of all birds, crows are also one of easiest for you to observe. No matter where you go, you are likely to see an American crow perched in a tree, flying overhead, or walking along the side of a road, and wherever crows go they bring their marvelous crow voices with them.

In fact, I have been routinely amazed at how many movies and dramatic television programs unintentionally feature the voices of crows in their soundtracks. Crows are very intelligent birds and they like to know what is going on around them. I imagine that the actors, actresses, cameras, and lighting of an outdoor movie set must be of great interest to them. As a result, the conversations of curious crows are often recorded along with the rest of the show.

Unfortunately, as the result of our shameful treatment of these wonderful birds, most crows will not allow humans to get close to them. Like ravens, crows have been shot, poisoned, and blown up for most all of our tenure here in the New World. The colorful array of Native American cultures which preceded our European presence actually liked and respected crows. The colonists, however, did not.

Crows are birds that flourish in a landscape comprised of a mixture of forests and fields. Human agricultural practices created such landscapes, and here in the Northeast, crows flourished. Unfortunately, crows make a living by eating anything they can find which is edible.

They will eat carrion, small mammals, small birds, and the eggs of almost any bird. Even today, crows have a very bad reputation as nest robbers, but their dietary habits never presented a problem to any bird population prior to our arrival here. We humans just don't like the idea very much.

Sport hunters in particular have been outraged that crows might be eating the eggs and young of ducks, geese, grouse, and other game birds. Consider this advertisement published by the American Game Protective Association, in 1920:

"This sable villain has some redeeming qualities. He sometimes feeds on harmful grubs and insects, but he also rouses the farmer's ire by pulling his corn. His greatest economic damage, however, is the home wrecking of game and insectivorous birds.

"Many of the game commissions are this year joining in a nationwide campaign against pernicious vermin — the destructive hawks and owls, cats, weasels, crows and the like. The sportsmen are being called upon to cooperate by using their guns against these enemies of game."

Once again, I am sickened. We now know that hawks and owls are beautiful and valuable animals to have around, as are the weasels and "cats." In this case, the cats being referred to were bobcats. The fact that the hunters of 1920 were being asked to protect ducks and geese from "economic" damage indicates that they had no real concern for the birds themselves, but rather the money the birds represented. They shot crows so that the helpless baby ducks and geese could grow up to be happy, healthy, and challenging targets for an afternoon of sport shooting.

Most upsetting, however, is the fact that there is still a regularly scheduled open season on crows. This byproduct of a bygone era allows licensed hunters to go out into the countryside from January to mid April, and then again from July to the end of December, and shoot as many crows as they can find. The break in the season is intended to allow crows to nest in peace. It just doesn't make any sense.

The only solace that I can offer you is that that the practice of crow hunting appears to be diminishing as hunters have let go of their prejudices against these wonderful, valuable birds.

The ultimate answer to the question, "What is the difference between a raven and a crow?" is this: American crows are basically small ravens. Whereas the scientific name of common ravens (*Covus corax*) means "The raven," the scientific name of the American crow (*Corvus brachyrhynchos*) means "The short-billed raven." Those fans of the etymology of words will be interested to learn that the species name *brachyrhynchos* is derived from the Greek words *brachys*, meaning "short" and *rhynchos*, meaning "beak."

Well, since there is still so much to tell you, I think that I will re-visit crows another time. This will give me a chance to tell you about the amazing social and family lives of these wonderful birds, and I may even be able to dig up some more information on the fish crow, whose scientific name (*Corvus ossifragus*) has the ominous meaning of, "the bone-breaking raven."

Lichens

H AVE YOU EVER SEEN A LICHEN? My guess is that you have and you didn't even notice. Lichens are all around us, living out their amazing lives in near-obscurity. If you don't think you've ever seen a lichen before then winter is actually a pretty good time to go out and look for one.

All you need to do is go for a walk in the woods, go cross country skiing down your favorite forest trail, or take a slow drive down a quiet street. Take a close look at the trunks of the trees which you pass and you will almost certainly notice a patch of mint-green material spread flat against the bark of a maple or other rough-barked tree. Should you find such an item growing on a tree then you can congratulate yourself. You will have found your very first lichen.

Lichens are the world's most resilient form of plant life, and certainly one of the strangest. What makes them so odd is the fact that they aren't simply plants, but rather a composite life form comprised of two very different types of plants — *algae* and *fungi*. They are the kind of hybrid life forms that science fiction stories are made of.

Before I go into too much detail on lichens, let me review their component parts. First we have the *algae* (pronounced AL-Gee). Perhaps the oldest form of plant life on earth, algae can be single celled plants that grow in your fish tank, or they can be huge, multicellular plants. The different seaweeds are actually forms of algae, with the 200-foot-long giant kelp being the largest.

Algae are capable of producing their own food through the process of photosynthesis. *Chlorophyll* gives them their green color, and all they need to survive is a sufficient supply of water, nutrients, and sunlight. Fungi are very different.

Unable to make their own food, all fungi are totally dependant on other living things for nourishment, much like animals. Some fungi have evolved to be parasitic, but most specialize in the consumption of dead plant and animal tissues, and they are the only reason that we are not all hip-deep in dead plants right now.

When most people think of fungi they probably think of mushrooms, but while all mushrooms are fungi, not all fungi have mushrooms. The thing about mushrooms is that they do not represent the entire plant of a given fungus.

Instead, think of a mushroom as an apple on an apple tree. Mushrooms are the reproductive bodies of certain fungi. The parent plants which gives rise to mushrooms are collections of root-like structures known as *hyphae* pronounced (HI-Fee.) These structures are usually concealed beneath the ground, or in rotting wood, and are rarely seen. Are you with me so far?

So, to visualize the structure of a lichen just think of the webs of hyphae which fungi are made of. Then imagine that your theoretical fungus is parasitic, living off other plants without fatally harming them. Now imagine that your fungus learns to capture and hold single celled alga plants inside the tangles of its hyphae. Your fungus has now equipped itself with little food factories and it no longer needs to rely on any other plant or animal for its survival. In short, your fungus has just become a lichen.

Many species of fungi have learned this trick. Since there are many different species of algae that can be held captive there are also many possible fungus-alga combinations, and thus, many species of lichens. The form of any given lichen is dependant upon which species of algae is being held by which species of fungus.

The most primitive lichens are little more than dry, flaky crusts that grow on rocks, and they are referred to as *crustose* lichens. The more complex *foliose* lichens have a leathery, leafy appearance and represent the next stage of lichen evolution. Finally, the most advanced *fruticose* lichens are quite similar in appearance to corals. They are best represented by the beautiful Scarlet Crested lichen *(Cladonia cristatella)*, which is more commonly known as "British Soldiers" in reference to the scarlet spore caps which are identical in color to the uniforms of the British "Red Coats."

The most amazing thing about the different species of lichens, however, is that none of the various fungi which hold algae as prisoners can be found growing in the wild. The evolutionary advantage was so great that the original parasitic, non-prisoner-holding fungi no longer exist. They are now so completely reliant on their algae that if you take any given lichen into a lab and separate the two plant forms, the fungi will die while the algae continue their existence as though nothing happened.

Oddly enough, however, the various lichen fungi don't seem to realize that they are so dependent on their respective algal prisoners. Each particular fungus will go about the business of producing spores, as seen clearly in the British Soldier lichen, even though the spores have little hope of survival in the absence of the required algae. The only way for lichens to reproduce is by breaking into pieces that then live as independent plants.

Before you start feeling too sorry for the algae which are in-corporated into lichens let me suggest that there are many advantages to being the prisoner of a fungus. All algae need water and in this respect lichen algae are pampered. The various lichen fungi are all experts at water retention, with certain species being able to absorb and hold so much water that they weigh 35 times more than they did when they were dry. Even in the driest places on Earth, lichen fungi have the ability to store water for years, slowly doling it out to the algae upon which they depend so much.

Lichen algae are also protected from the harshest temperatures imaginable. If, for instance, you were to climb to the top of New Hampshire's Mt. Washington in winter you would be subjected to temperatures of $-30°$ F and wind chills in excess of $-100°$ F. You would also find that you were surrounded by a thriving community of lichens.

On the other end of the temperature gradient, lichens have be brought into laboratory settings and exposed to temperatures of $268°$ Celsius for several hours. After being given the chance to cool down, the lichens resumed their normal metabolisms with no sign of damage. There appears to be no naturally occurring temperature too cold or too hot for lichens to endure.

The marvels of lichen survival are all due to the impressive abilities of the lichen fungi, which grow thick-walled, gelatinous cells that can shield the lichen algae from almost any environmental condition. The lichen algae are provided with special chambers just below this protective wall where light can easily reach them. All the algae need to do is produce food, the fungi to the rest of the work.

The fungi of the rock-loving lichens have another impressive ability. Strong acids produced within the fungal cells are actually able to dissolve rock, freeing up the minerals and nutrients which the algae plants need for photosynthesis. This is how lichens are able to live on top of bare mountains, the sides of buildings, or on gravestones in cemeteries.

Only fire, pollution, and competition with higher order plants can kill lichens. Left alone, individual lichens may well live for thousands of years. So the next time you see a lichen don't just pass it by. Stop and take a good look. It may have been around for a long time.

Cattails

DECEMBER IS A QUIET MONTH. Find yourself an old stump, a fallen log, or even just a nice quiet place to stand for a while and I am sure that you will notice your thoughts starting to wander. Where have you been? Where are you going? Two short questions — one easy to answer and the other almost impossible.

Now I can't really explain why, but I find myself drawn to ponds in the winter. It might be because I simply like ponds, or it might be because ponds are such a contradiction in the winter. Think of a pond and what do you se in your mind's eye? I see warm, fluid, aromatic water. Yet when I walk down to the local pond during the winter I will find a hard, unyielding sheet of ice — a pond that isn't a pond.

But there are signs that a fluid pond was there earlier in the year. Actually, there are many such signs, but none are more powerful than cattails. During the winter, when ponds and marshes are asleep, cattails are easily accessible to humans. After a prolonged period of sub-zero temperatures you can simply venture out across the ice and walk through the remnants of these sturdy wetland plants. This is actually a really great place to set up a folding chair and sit for a while.

As you settle in to do some sitting you will have a perspective that humans rarely get to enjoy. You will be in a complex habitat that most of us don't venture into during the warmer months (mostly because we don't often enjoy sinking up to our armpits in mud). So why don't you give it a try? Keep in mind that you have to let a safe layer of ice form first! While you're walking out onto the pond I'll share a few tidbits about cattails with you.

The cattail family is a small one. There are only 18 species worldwide, and all of them are found in the same genus. In the northeastern part of the United States you are only likely to encounter 2 of the 18 species: the Common or Broad-leaved Cattail (*Typha latifolia*) and the Narrow-leaved Cattail (*T. angustifolia*).

As you may have surmised already, the two species are very similar in appearance. In addition to slight differences in leaf width the species' stems and flowers also differ along similar lines. The narrow-leaved cattail has a very slender spike of flowers, which will eventually become the dark-brown seedhead that resembles a sausage. Narrow-leaved cattails are more coastal in their distribution, however.

By the way, it may interest you to know that the big brown sausage-shaped seedhead is actually what remains of the female flower of a cattail. In the spring, the male flowers are located in a smaller golden spike just above the female flowers. They wither shortly after releasing their pollen, but you can still see the long needle-like stem that sticks up above the female flower through most of the year.

The female flowers, which start out as green as the leaves, start to ripen and turn brown after they are fertilized. Believe it or not, these flowers can produce up to 220,000 seeds! The seeds are ridiculously small and are attached to feathery down that can carry them from one wetland area to another on even a gentle breeze. They also make a satisfactory explosion of fluff if you throw one at a friend! Or should I say ". . ." if you energetically attempt to share one of Nature's wonders with a beloved companion?

Cattails are used by a wide variety of birds, mammals, and insects. Beavers and muskrats eat the nutritious roots, and muskrats build their domed houses primarily out of cattail leaves. Birds don't eat the leaves or the seeds, which are simply too small to bother with, but they do make use of the cattails' location for nestbuilding. Swamp sparrows, marsh wrens, and red-winged blackbirds are all regular nest-builders in cattail stands, but there is another resource that cattails offer indirectly to birds — food. Birds can't eat cattails, but there are many species of insects that can. Aphids suck juices from the stems and beetle grubs bore into the stems and eat the fleshy bits.

Of course there are other insects and spiders that eat the aphids and beetles, and birds will eat all of them. The wrens, blackbirds, and sparrows may abandon the cattails during the winter, but there are a couple of our winter resident birds that will venture out into the marshes to feed on these "bugs" during the colder months. Chief among them are downy woodpeckers and our dear little friends the black-capped chickadees.

Cattails are some of the most thought-provoking plants I know of. Whenever I wander out into a thick patch of winter cattails I find that my imagination really starts working. Echoes of the pond's former glory and shades of its promising future, cattails simply make time go by in my head. Let me see if I can show you what I mean.

Imagine a spot near the margin of a pond where the cattails aren't too thick. There are little corridors running between the golden leaves and stems — pathways that would be perfect for a person on skates to explore, but that's not what I see in my head. Instead I move forward in time to early spring.

I see a mallard swimming through the channels looking for food after a long flight. The muddy shore nearby may even be the temporary home of a spotted sandpiper that has just returned from its wintering grounds, and there's always a chance that you'll see a beaver digging for fresh cattail roots in the shallows.

As time goes by the cattail leaves start to emerge from the mud. The previous year's leaves are still evident, but they are now dry and faded — perfect nesting material for grebes, bitterns, coots, rails, and ducks. It will be a while before the new cattails reach their full height, but when they do they will provide nest locations and materials for wrens, sparrows, and red-winged blackbirds.

Frogs and toads will sing among the cattails and attach their eggs, in masses or strings, in the safe waters between the cattail stems. Small fish will hunt for food and hide from predators in these thickets, and dragonfly nymphs will ascend the broad, green leaves to hatch from their shells and take wing for the first time.

By the time little ducklings are following their mothers down the cattail channels there will be an entire host of birds living in, and around, the marshy margins of the pond. Many birds cannot nest in the cattails, but they still visit them to collect that wonderfully soft cattail down that will make the linings of their nests so warm and soft. And all the while, baby red-winged blackbirds sit and think their little blackbird thoughts while they wait for their fathers to bring them some food. I bet you have already forgotten that I am actually sitting in a folding chair on the ice covering a winter pond. It happens to me all the time.